embroidered
wild flowers

Patterns Inspired by Field and Forest

KAZUKO
AOKI

ROOST BOOKS
Boulder 2020

Contents

when the dandelions bloom

Warmed by the sunshine, the dandelions grow taller and their yellow flowers open. In a matter of time, the dandelions' fluff takes flight, steadily expanding their domain.

See page 54

walking along the embankment

Fertile stem

Field horsetail

Walking along the sunny embankment, the tiny flowers of early spring are everywhere—field horsetails and their fertile stems, along with rapeseed blossoms and Persian speedwell.

See page 56

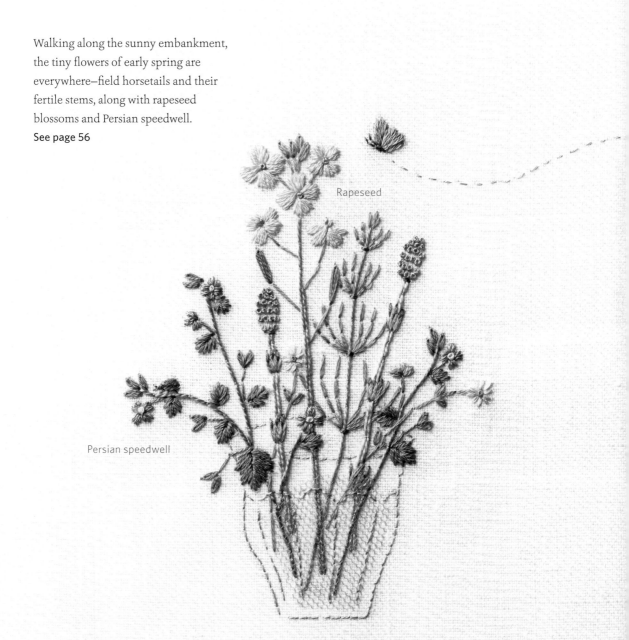

Rapeseed

Persian speedwell

long-headed poppies

Although the poppy is an exotic plant species, somewhere along the line these flowers have become a staple of the spring landscape.
See page 58

11

violets

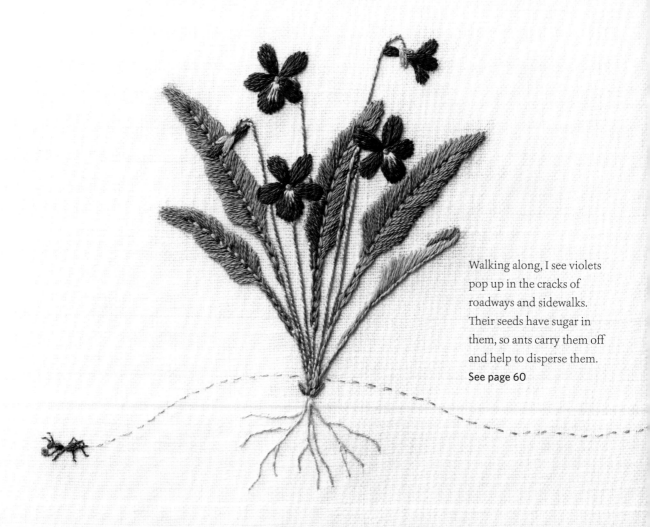

Walking along, I see violets pop up in the cracks of roadways and sidewalks. Their seeds have sugar in them, so ants carry them off and help to disperse them.

See page 60

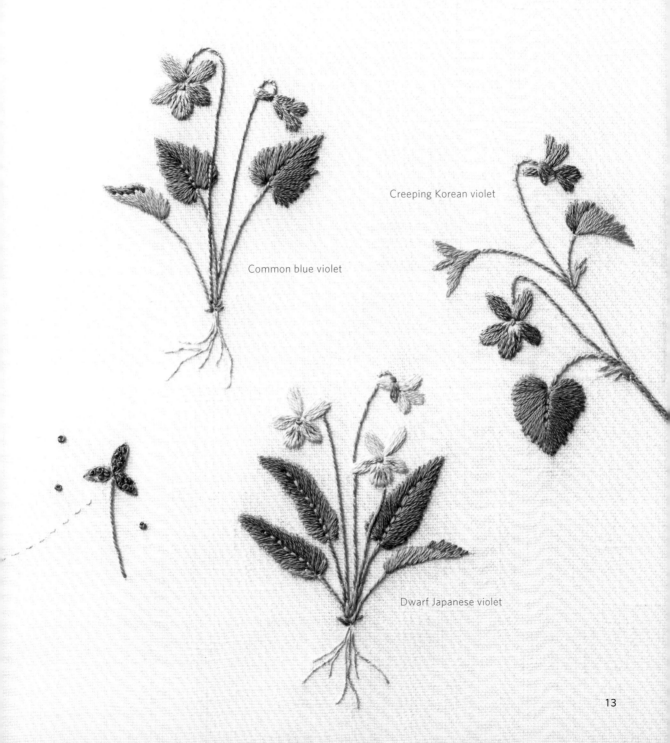

Creeping Korean violet

Common blue violet

Dwarf Japanese violet

13

spring paths

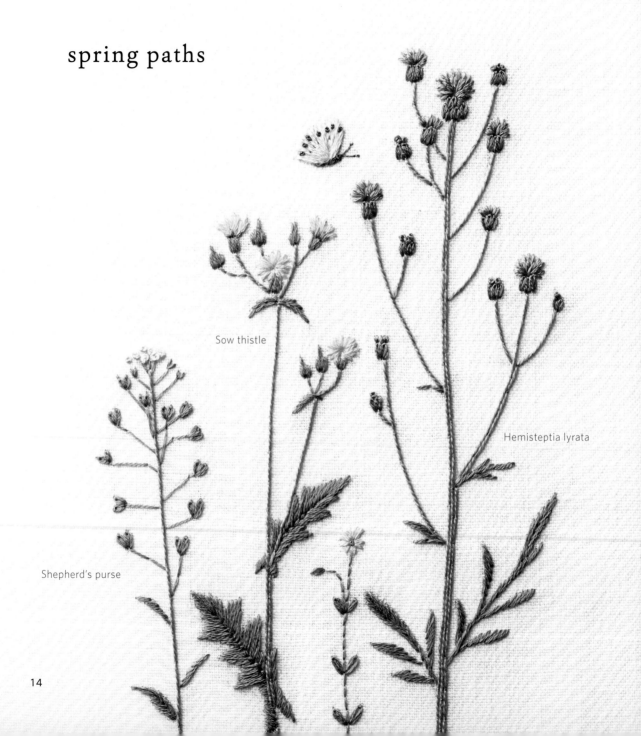

Sow thistle

Hemisteptia lyrata

Shepherd's purse

These are some of my favorite places where spring flowers bloom.
See page 62

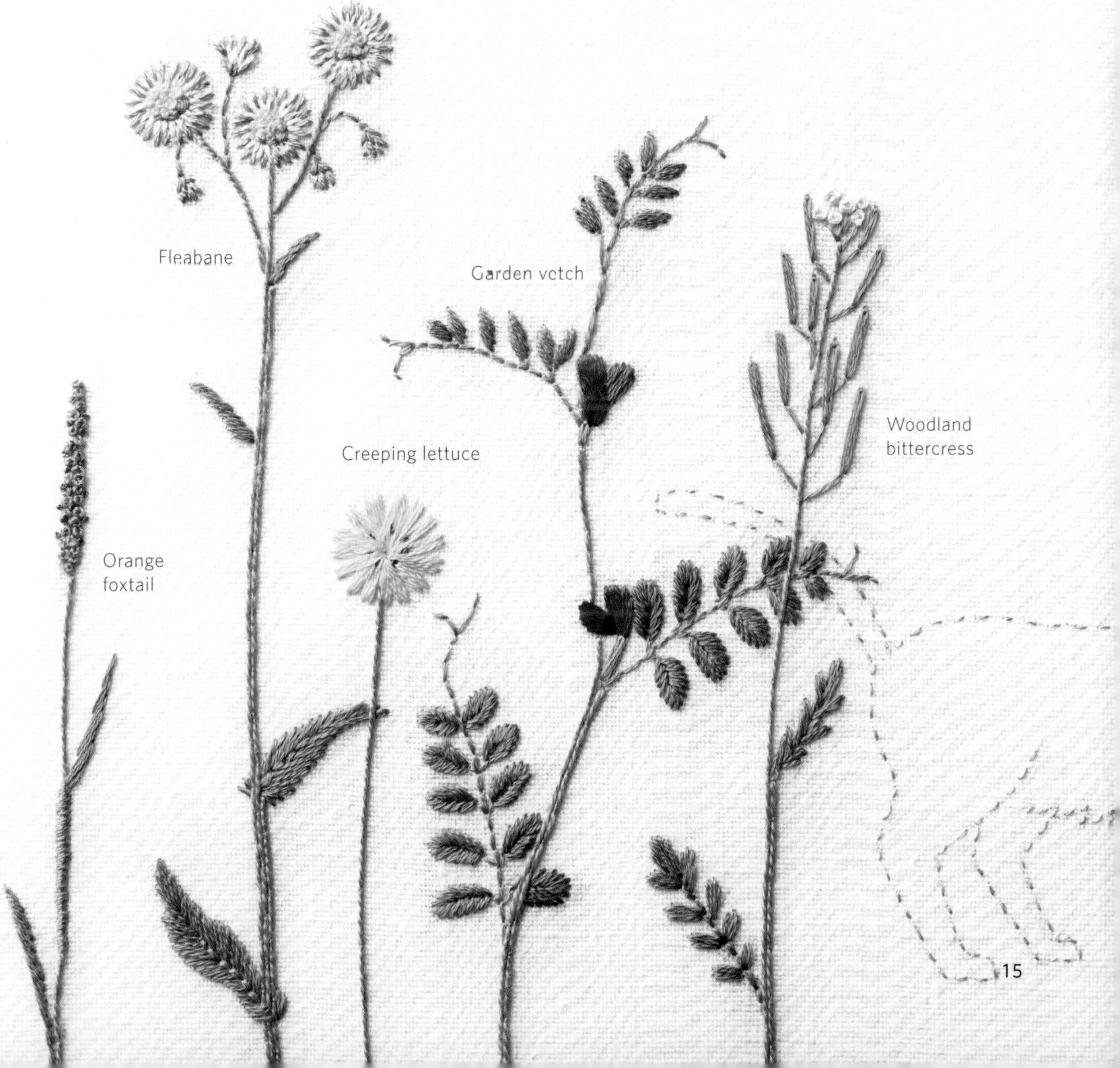

Fleabane

Garden vetch

Creeping lettuce

Woodland bittercress

Orange foxtail

Maple raspberry

wild raspberry & mock strawberry

Mock strawberry

Wild raspberry

Various kinds of wild Japanese berries grow on the edges of the woods. I even find Japanese brambles at the sides of railroad crossings, and every year I look forward to seeing them on my travels.

See page 64

Japanese bramble

rainy days

One of the pleasures of the rainy season is the blooming of the hydrangeas. One of the many varieties is the Tea of Heaven hydrangea, which has diminutive petals.

See page 66

Tea of Heaven hydrangea

sunflowers in array

The sunflowers that thrive along the paths
between rice paddies can grow so tall you have
to look up at them. Sometimes their heads
droop in the heat of the afternoon sun.

See page 68

flowering grasses

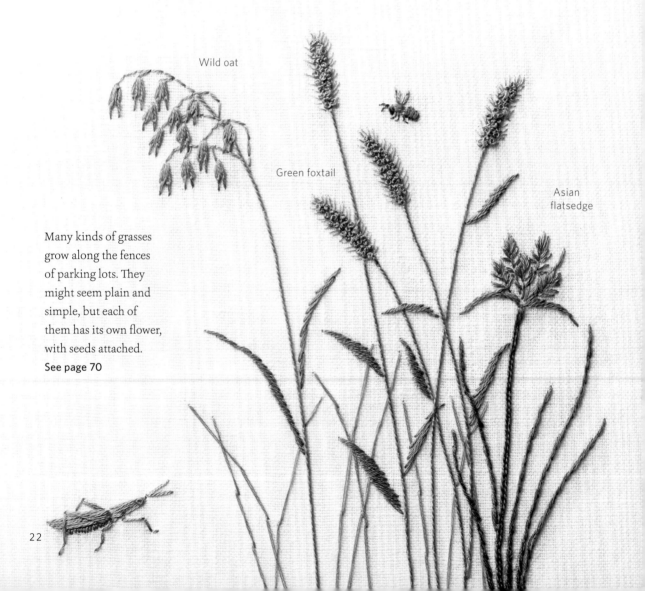

Wild oat

Green foxtail

Asian flatsedge

Many kinds of grasses grow along the fences of parking lots. They might seem plain and simple, but each of them has its own flower, with seeds attached.

See page 70

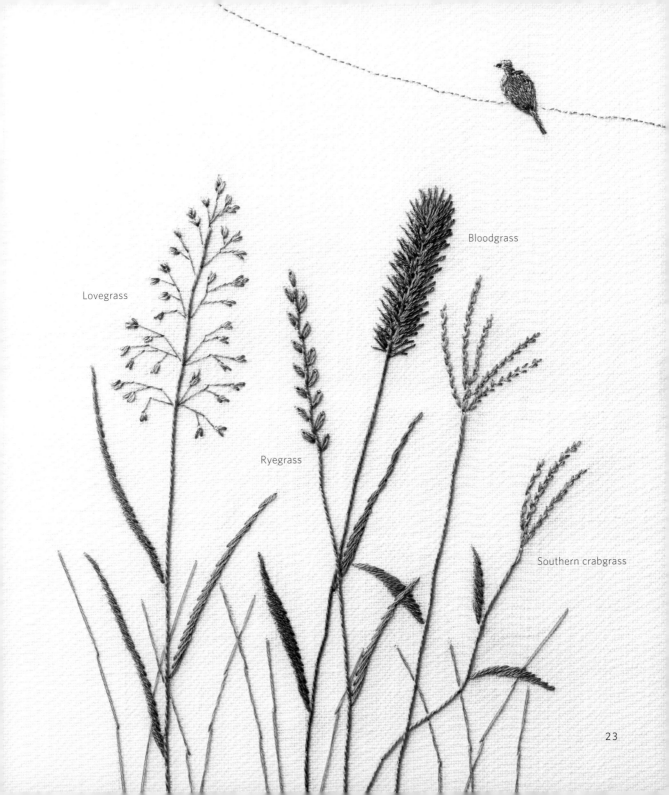

Lovegrass

Bloodgrass

Ryegrass

Southern crabgrass

in the corners of the garden

The garden corners where the cicadas sing
are an oasis of wild flowers and grasses.
They creep over the grounds, growing in
clumps and spreading their tendrils. And
then insects take up residence there too.

See page 24

Creeping woodsorrel

Prostrate spurge

Skunkvine

Asiatic dayflower

Chameleon plant

25

summer's butterflies

On days of blazing sunshine, swallowtails flit back and forth in the shade.
See page 74

Old world swallowtail

Pea blue

Asian comma

Small copper

Eastern pale
clouded yellow

Small cabbage
white

autumn paths

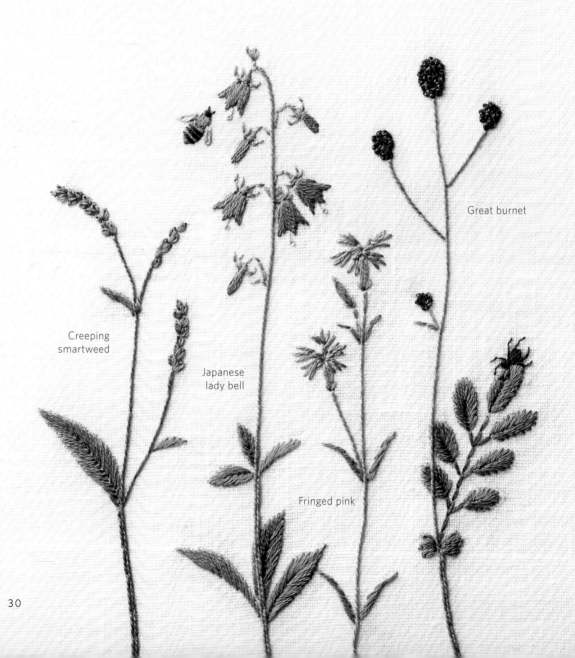

Great burnet

Creeping
smartweed

Japanese
lady bell

Fringed pink

As the heat relents and the breeze grows cooler,
these flowers bloom at the edges of the woods
and at the bases of the pampas grasses.

See page 76

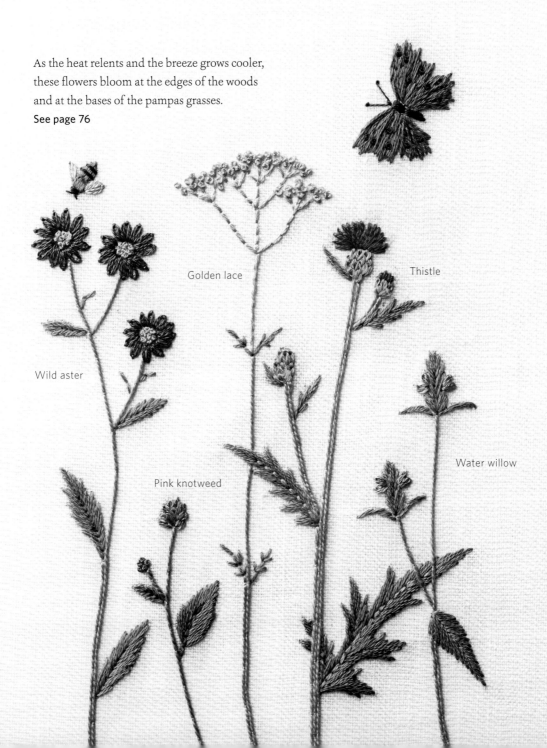

Golden lace

Thistle

Wild aster

Water willow

Pink knotweed

colorful changing leaves

See page 78

Sweetgum

Mountain cherry

Gingko

Chinese tallow

32

Konara oak

Trident maple

American sycamore

forest combing

Whether in nearby woods or distant forests, these are the mushrooms I always hope to encounter. **See page 80**

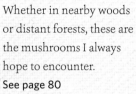

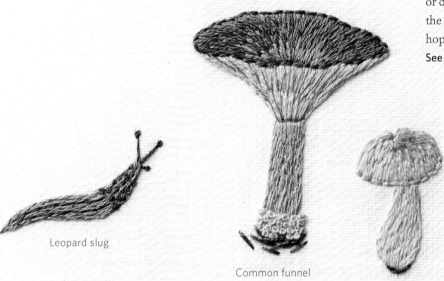

Leopard slug

Common funnel

Sulfur tuft

Fly agaric

White dunce cap

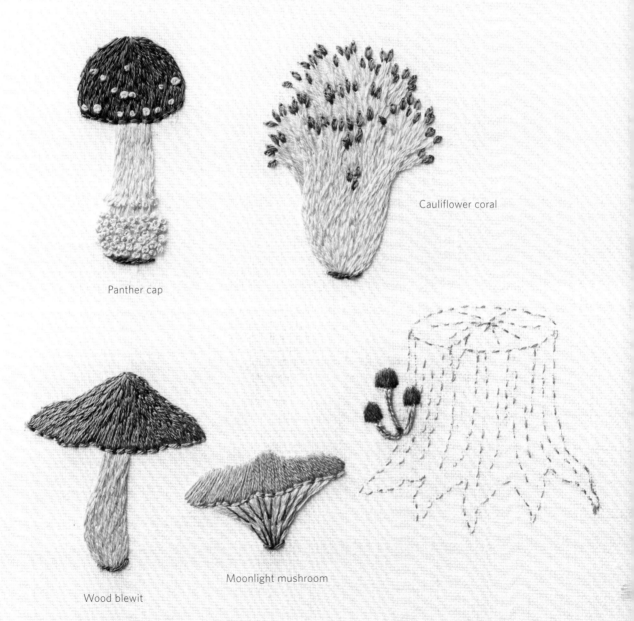

Panther cap

Cauliflower coral

Wood blewit

Moonlight mushroom

the opposite bank of the canal

Although I've never been
to the Netherlands, this
is what I imagine the late
autumn landscape looks
like along the canals.
See page 88

bird watching

See page 84

Sparrow

Pygmy woodpecker

Daurian redstart

Red-flanked bluetail

Brown-eared bulbul

mistletoe

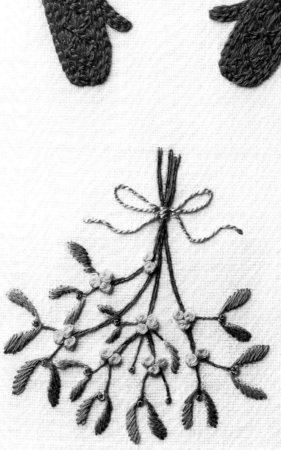

A friend who lives nearby delivered some mistletoe along with a gift from another friend who lives in Yatsugatake.

See page 86

collecting materials

I like to make a wreath
with wisteria vines and
attach materials I've
gathered. Bring a basket
with you on your walks.
See page 88

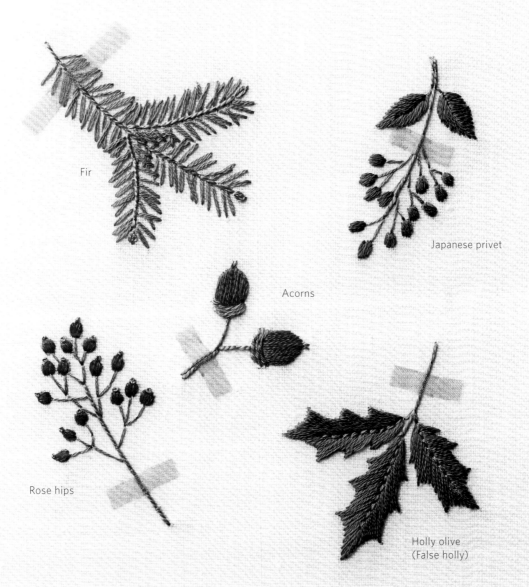

Fir

Japanese privet

Acorns

Rose hips

Holly olive
(False holly)

the world of mosses

Silvergreen bryum moss

Juniper haircap moss

Leucobryum bowringii

Once you start looking for it, you'll find that moss is every-where. At the edge of the road or at the foot of a tree, and mosses have flowers that bloom too.
See page 90

Common liverwort

Common apple-moss

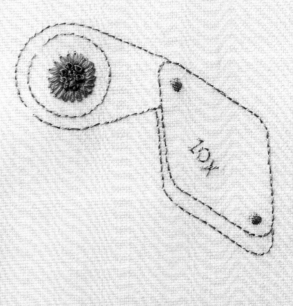

objects that are rather
ordinary but still special

These objects are perfectly
ordinary, but that's exactly
what makes them special. Pick
them up and hold them in your
hand, and you'll understand.

See page 92

How to make

when working in embroidery

EMBROIDERY FLOSS AND THREAD In this book, I mainly use DMC embroidery floss. For DMC No. 5 and for linen thread, I embroider with a single strand. DMC No. 25 is sold loosely plied in 6 strands, so first I cut it to the length I will use—I find that about 50 to 60 cm is easiest to work with—and then I pull out the necessary number of strands, one by one, and reassemble them. I embroider with 3 strands, unless noted otherwise.

For instructions that use the term "variegated," I embroider with 2 or more colors threaded on the same needle. Blending colors is an effective way to add intensity and depth.

For projects in this book that call for a couching stitch, I use 1, 2, or 3 strands of No. 25 unless specified otherwise; sometimes I call for No. 5 or linen thread. So as not to call attention to the No. 5 laid thread, I use a single strand of No. 25 in the same color to fasten it in place. When using linen thread for the laid thread, I use a single strand of No. 25 in a similar color to fasten it in place.

EMBROIDERY NEEDLES The correlation between embroidery thread and needle is very important. Choose an appropriate needle according to the weight of the thread, and always use sharp needles.

DMC No. 5, single strand
French embroidery needle No. 3 or 4

DMC No. 25, 2 or 3 strands
French embroidery needle No. 7

DMC No. 25, single strand
Thin sewing needle

Linen embroidery thread, single strand
French embroidery needle No. 7

EMBROIDERY FABRIC For projects in this book, I worked in the center of a 35 cm x 30 cm piece of 100% linen, on a Bunka Embroidery #1 frame (24 cm x 19 cm).

Always apply single-sided fusible interfacing (midweight) to the reverse side of the fabric before embroidering. This application reduces the amount the fabric stretches, prevents the stitches on the reverse side from pulling on the front, and dramatically improves the look of the finished product.

EMBROIDERY PATTERNS Patterns are printed actual size. To transfer the pattern to your fabric, first copy it to tracing paper. Then, layer water-soluble Chaco paper (I recommend using gray), the tracing paper with the pattern, and cellophane on the right side of the fabric. Use a craft stylus to transfer the pattern to the fabric.

EMBROIDERY FRAMES When working embroidery, stretching fabric on a frame is a beautiful way to finish a project. For smaller projects, use a circular hoop; for larger projects, use a rectangular frame in a size that corresponds to the project.

TIPS AND TRICKS

- When embroidering, transfer the pattern to the fabric, as described above. Depending upon the fabric you use, sometimes all of the details don't transfer—in that case, add them in with a ballpoint pen (make sure the ink can be erased with heat later). Properly transferring your pattern is the key to creating beautiful embroidery.

- When finishing your project, first spray it with water, erase the lines from the Chaco paper, then apply heat to the reverse side of the fabric with an iron or a hairdryer to remove the pen lines.

- Embroider in this order for plants: stem > leaf > flower. Adding the veins of the leaves at the end will give your stitches a pleasantly fluffy appearance.

- For leaves and flowers, work the embroidery from the outside toward the center.

- I did my best to make these patterns and instructions easy to follow, but before you begin embroidering, I recommend taking a look at the real thing—whether in photographs in a field guide or on the Internet—in order to reinforce your image of what it should look like. This will make it easier to express yourself in your work, and you won't ever doubt your stitches.

- The many varieties of plants and birds each have their own characteristics, and no two are alike. Embroider more flowers, or make the birds even softer and fuller—have fun with it!

stitch catalog

NOTE: In the embroidery patterns, the stitch names are shortened to just their main name. For example, if a running stitch is indicated, it will be noted simply as "Running."

RUNNING STITCH Use a running stitch when you want to add a stitch but you want it to be inconspicuous.

BACK STITCH A back stitch produces neat and cleanly finished line of stitching. When working along a curve, make fine stitches. I use this stitch for leaf designs and the tips of stems.

OUTLINE STITCH An outline stitch creates line stitching that has volume and texture. You can also use this stitch to create a surface of stitches next to each other, such as those used to create stems and roots.

COUCHING STITCH A couching stitch is a good choice for embroidering fine lettering because you can freestyle your own lines. Or use this stitch to create a vigorous stem with No. 5 floss. Work compact laid stitches for a beautiful finish.

STRAIGHT STITCH A straight stitch is a simple stitch, but it can make your embroidery come alive. Use it to work fine petals or the details on a plant.

SPLIT STITCH I often use a split stitch to work a surface of stitches next to each other. Even on broad leaves, where the stitches overlap, this stitch is not bulky. Use a slightly longer needle for a flat finish.

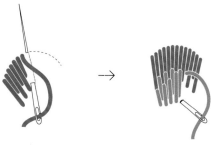

LONG AND SHORT STITCH I often use this stitch for broad areas. Be sure to work stitches by bringing the needle up from somewhere outside the pattern line and then coming back down inside the line.

When working a second row of stitches, bring the needle up between the threads from the first row to prevent any gaps in your stitches.

SATIN STITCH A satin stitch is a perfect stitch for the flat and shiny aspect of flower petals. You can also use it for leaves. Create a nice finish by pulling all the stitches at the same tension.

FRENCH KNOT STITCH (shown with 2 wraps) Use French knots for flower centers, small buds, or seeds. Knots can appear stiff or soft, depending on the tension of the thread. In this book, work with 2 wraps unless specified otherwise.

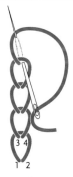

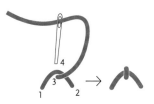

CHAIN STITCH Use a chain stitch to create line stitching that has volume by working a thin chain of tightly pulled stitches.

FLY STITCH Use a fly stitch for the wings of birds or butterflies. You can create a different effect depending on the anchor stitch.

51

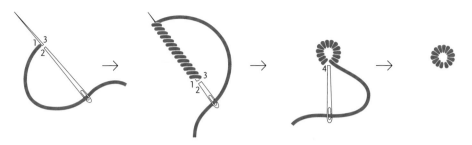

BULLION STITCH (COIL) Use a bullion stitch for a coiled finished shape. Bring the needle up a short distance between 2 and 3 in the fabric, and wrap the thread around the needle enough times to cover the circumference of the circle, then pull the needle through the coil, wrap the coil into a circle, and bring the needle back down through the fabric.

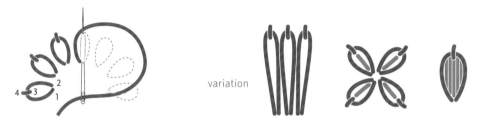

variation

LAZY DAISY STITCH Use a lazy daisy stitch for small petals or calyxes. You can also combine it with a straight stitch or satin stitch to fill in the middle of a shape. Adjust the shape by shifting the tension of the thread.

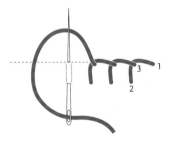

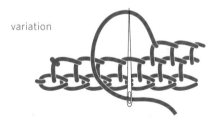

variation

BLANKET STITCH A blanket stitch is often used for appliqués or edging. Adjust the space between or the length of the stitches to suit the pattern. This stitch is also called a buttonhole stitch.

Work a row of chain stitches, then insert the needle into each chain stitch below as you work the blanket stitches above it. For additional rows, stagger the stitches.

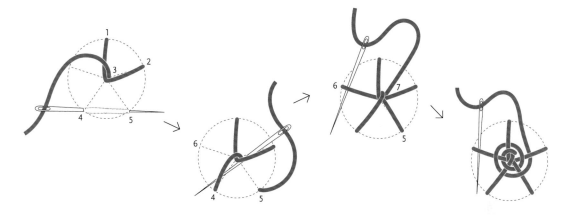

SPIDER WEB STITCH (shown with 5 spokes) Make 5 straight stitches, radiating from the center of a circular shape. Then bring the thread up at the center and coil it around, alternating over and under the radial stitches.

HOW TO MAKE THE LEAVES ON THE PROSTRATE SPURGE page 72

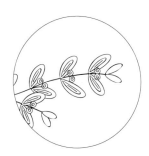

Work the inner lazy daisy stitch, then work the outer double stitch, and fill in with a straight stitch. If you make the anchor stitches small, it creates a rounded leaf tip.

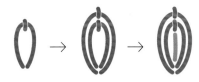

HOW TO MAKE THE BIRDS' EYES page 84

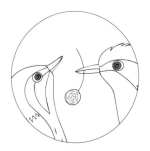

First work a French knot stitch, then enclose it with a fine white line by working a 1-strand lazy daisy stitch. Create a different effect with the inner and outer corners of the eyes, depending upon which side you place the anchor stitches and how much space you leave for the lazy daisy stitch.

when the dandelions bloom page 6

MATERIALS DMC embroidery floss No. 25
(989, 988, 3346, 726, 3821, 729, 613, 3863, 168,
844, 3023); DMC embroidery floss No. 5 (989)

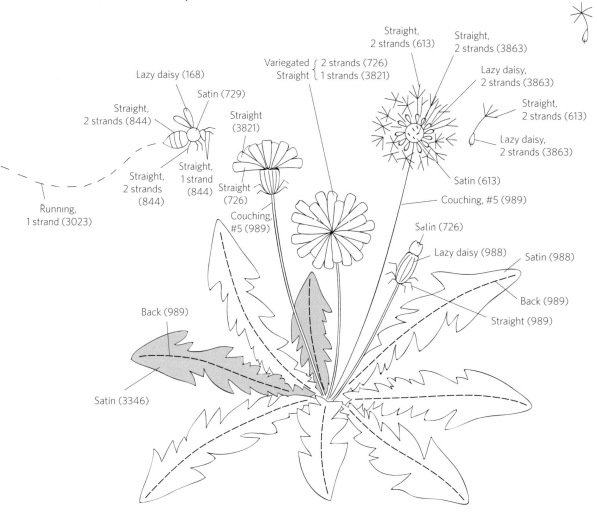

Straight,
2 strands (613)

Straight,
2 strands (3863)

Variegated ⎰ 2 strands (726)
Straight ⎱ 1 strands (3821)

Lazy daisy,
2 strands (3863)

Lazy daisy (168)

Satin (729)

Straight,
2 strands (613)

Straight,
2 strands (844)

Straight
(3821)

Lazy daisy,
2 strands (3863)

Straight,
1 strand
(844)

Satin (613)

Straight,
2 strands
(844)

Straight
(726)

Couching, #5 (989)

Running,
1 strand (3023)

Couching,
#5 (989)

Satin (726)

Lazy daisy (988)

Satin (988)

Back (989)

Back (989)

Straight (989)

Satin (3346)

Straight,
2 strands (613)

Lazy daisy,
2 strands (3863)

MATERIALS DMC embroidery floss No. 25 (989, 988, 726, 613, 3863); DMC embroidery floss No. 5 (989); Polyester tulle scraps (green), as needed; invisible thread

French knot (726)
Work a combination of 1 to 3 wraps

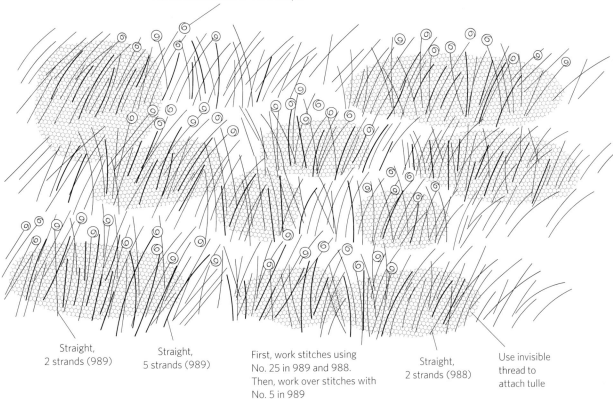

Straight,
2 strands (989)

Straight,
5 strands (989)

First, work stitches using
No. 25 in 989 and 988.
Then, work over stitches with
No. 5 in 989

Straight,
2 strands (988)

Use invisible
thread to
attach tulle

walking along the embankment page 8

MATERIALS DMC embroidery floss No.
25 (989, 3347, 372, 611, 422, 822, 3023);
DMC embroidery floss No. 5 (738, 989)

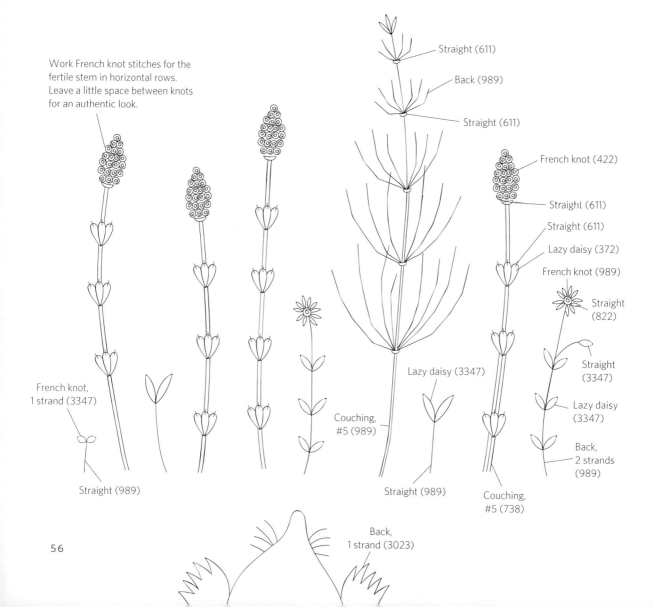

Work French knot stitches for the
fertile stem in horizontal rows.
Leave a little space between knots
for an authentic look.

Straight (611)

Back (989)

Straight (611)

French knot (422)

Straight (611)

Straight (611)

Lazy daisy (372)

French knot (989)

Straight
(822)

Lazy daisy (3347)

Straight
(3347)

French knot,
1 strand (3347)

Lazy daisy
(3347)

Couching,
#5 (989)

Back,
2 strands
(989)

Straight (989)

Straight (989)

Couching,
#5 (738)

Back,
1 strand (3023)

MATERIALS DMC embroidery floss No. 25 (989, 988, 3347, 372, 3012, 611, 422, 3822, 3328, 156, 822, 3023, 645); DMC embroidery floss No. 5 (738, 989, 3012); Polyester tulle scraps (blue-gray)

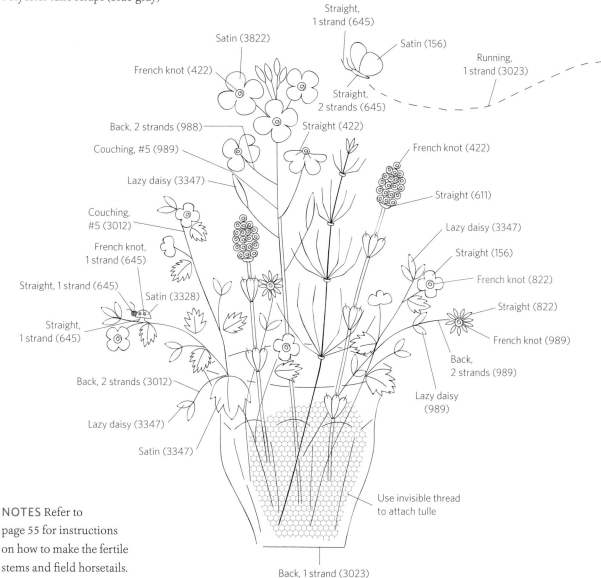

Satin (3822)

French knot (422)

Straight, 1 strand (645)

Satin (156)

Running, 1 strand (3023)

Straight, 2 strands (645)

Back, 2 strands (988)

Straight (422)

Couching, #5 (989)

French knot (422)

Lazy daisy (3347)

Straight (611)

Couching, #5 (3012)

Lazy daisy (3347)

Straight (156)

French knot, 1 strand (645)

French knot (822)

Straight, 1 strand (645)

Straight (822)

Satin (3328)

French knot (989)

Straight, 1 strand (645)

Back, 2 strands (989)

Back, 2 strands (3012)

Lazy daisy (989)

Lazy daisy (3347)

Satin (3347)

Use invisible thread to attach tulle

NOTES Refer to page 55 for instructions on how to make the fertile stems and field horsetails.

Back, 1 strand (3023)

long-headed poppies page 10

MATERIALS DMC embroidery floss No. 25
(989, 3347, 3012, 721, 351, 3866, 738, 844);
DMC embroidery floss No. 5 (989)

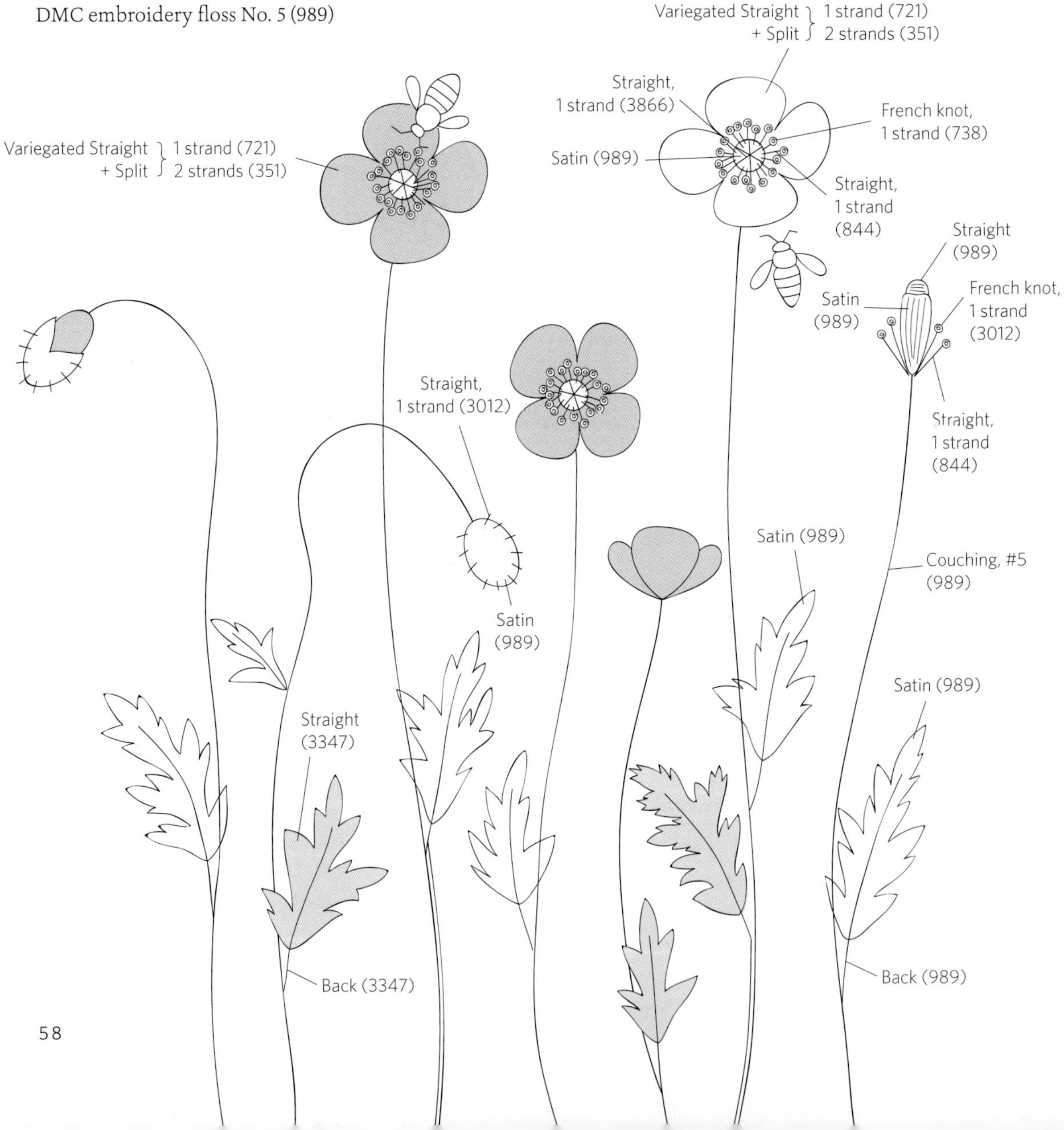

Variegated Straight ⎱ 1 strand (721)
+ Split ⎰ 2 strands (351)

Straight,
1 strand (3866)

French knot,
1 strand (738)

Satin (989)

Straight,
1 strand
(844)

Straight
(989)

French knot,
1 strand
(3012)

Satin
(989)

Variegated Straight ⎱ 1 strand (721)
+ Split ⎰ 2 strands (351)

Straight,
1 strand (3012)

Straight,
1 strand
(844)

Satin
(989)

Satin (989)

Couching, #5
(989)

Satin (989)

Straight
(3347)

Back (3347)

Back (989)

MATERIALS DMC embroidery floss No. 25 (989, 3347, 3012, 721, 351, 729, 844, 168); DMC embroidery floss No. 5 (989, 3012)

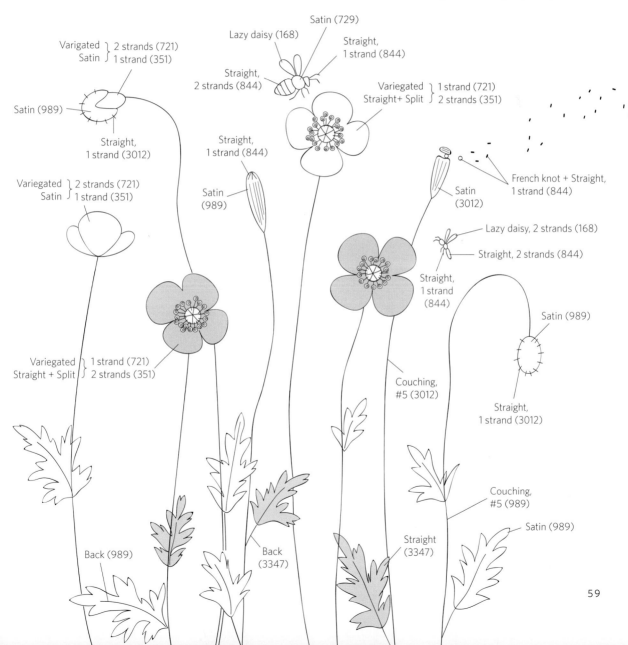

Varigated Satin } 2 strands (721) 1 strand (351)

Satin (989)

Straight, 1 strand (3012)

Lazy daisy (168)

Satin (729)

Straight, 1 strand (844)

Straight, 2 strands (844)

Variegated Straight + Split } 1 strand (721) 2 strands (351)

French knot + Straight, 1 strand (844)

Variegated Satin } 2 strands (721) 1 strand (351)

Straight, 1 strand (844)

Satin (989)

Satin (3012)

Lazy daisy, 2 strands (168)

Straight, 2 strands (844)

Straight, 1 strand (844)

Satin (989)

Variegated Straight + Split } 1 strand (721) 2 strands (351)

Couching, #5 (3012)

Straight, 1 strand (3012)

Couching, #5 (989)

Satin (989)

Back (989)

Back (3347)

Straight (3347)

violets _{page 12}

MATERIALS DMC embroidery floss No. 25 (368, 989, 3347, 3363, 3820, 333, 3837, 3862, 3865, 3023, 844, 613); DMC embroidery floss No. 5 (989, 841); Art Fiber Endo linen embroidery thread (L901)

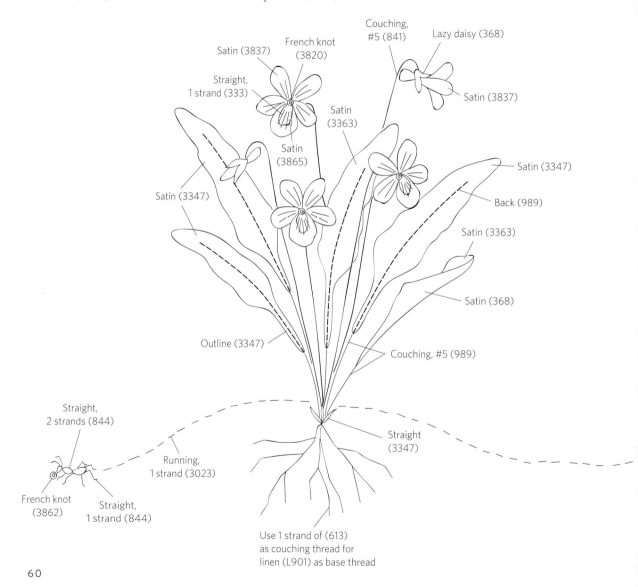

Couching, #5 (841)

Lazy daisy (368)

French knot (3820)

Satin (3837)

Straight, 1 strand (333)

Satin (3363)

Satin (3837)

Satin (3865)

Satin (3347)

Back (989)

Satin (3347)

Satin (3363)

Satin (368)

Outline (3347)

Couching, #5 (989)

Straight, 2 strands (844)

Straight (3347)

Running, 1 strand (3023)

French knot (3862)

Straight, 1 strand (844)

Use 1 strand of (613) as couching thread for linen (L901) as base thread

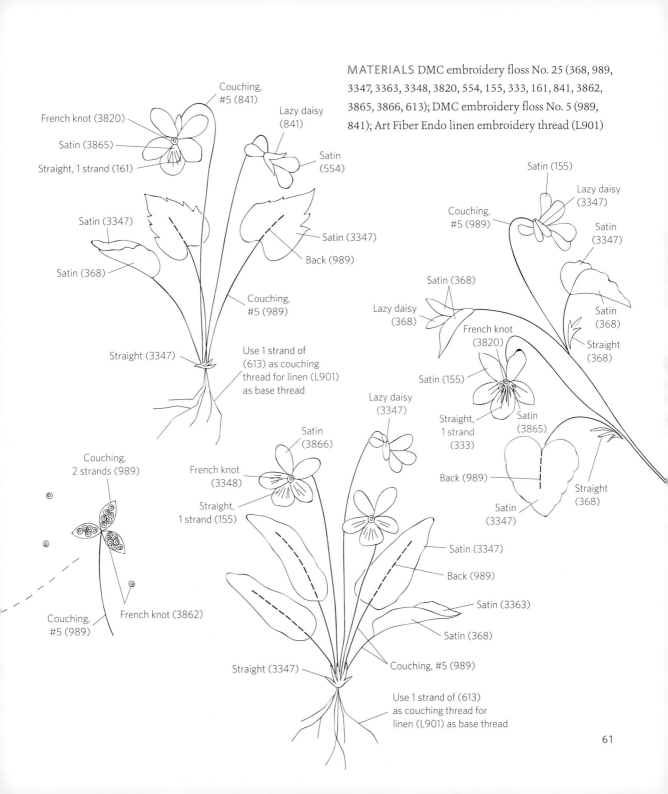

Couching, #5 (841)

French knot (3820)

Satin (3865)

Straight, 1 strand (161)

Lazy daisy (841)

Satin (554)

MATERIALS DMC embroidery floss No. 25 (368, 989, 3347, 3363, 3348, 3820, 554, 155, 333, 161, 841, 3862, 3865, 3866, 613); DMC embroidery floss No. 5 (989, 841); Art Fiber Endo linen embroidery thread (L901)

Satin (155)

Lazy daisy (3347)

Couching, #5 (989)

Satin (3347)

Satin (3347)

Back (989)

Satin (3347)

Satin (368)

Couching, #5 (989)

Satin (368)

Satin (368)

Straight (3347)

Use 1 strand of (613) as couching thread for linen (L901) as base thread

Lazy daisy (368)

French knot (3820)

Satin (155)

Straight, 1 strand (333)

Satin (3865)

Back (989)

Satin (3347)

Straight (368)

Straight (368)

Couching, 2 strands (989)

Lazy daisy (3347)

Satin (3866)

French knot (3348)

Straight, 1 strand (155)

Couching, #5 (989)

French knot (3862)

Satin (3347)

Back (989)

Satin (3363)

Satin (368)

Couching, #5 (989)

Straight (3347)

Use 1 strand of (613) as couching thread for linen (L901) as base thread

spring paths page 14

MATERIALS DMC embroidery floss No. 25 (470, 989, 988, 320, 554, 726, ECRU, 3863, 646); DMC embroidery floss No. 5 (989)

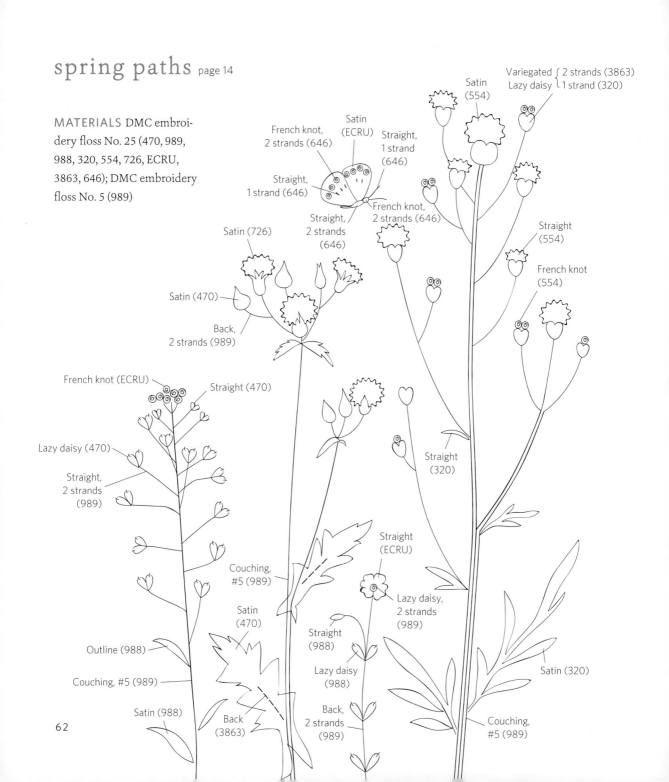

Satin (554)

Variegated ⎧ 2 strands (3863)
Lazy daisy ⎩ 1 strand (320)

French knot, 2 strands (646)

Satin (ECRU)

Straight, 1 strand (646)

Straight, 1 strand (646)

French knot, 2 strands (646)

Straight, 2 strands (646)

Straight (554)

French knot (554)

Satin (726)

Satin (470)

Back, 2 strands (989)

French knot (ECRU)

Straight (470)

Straight (320)

Lazy daisy (470)

Straight, 2 strands (989)

Straight (ECRU)

Couching, #5 (989)

Satin (470)

Lazy daisy, 2 strands (989)

Straight (988)

Outline (988)

Lazy daisy (988)

Couching, #5 (989)

Satin (320)

Satin (988)

Back (3863)

Back, 2 strands (989)

Couching, #5 (989)

62

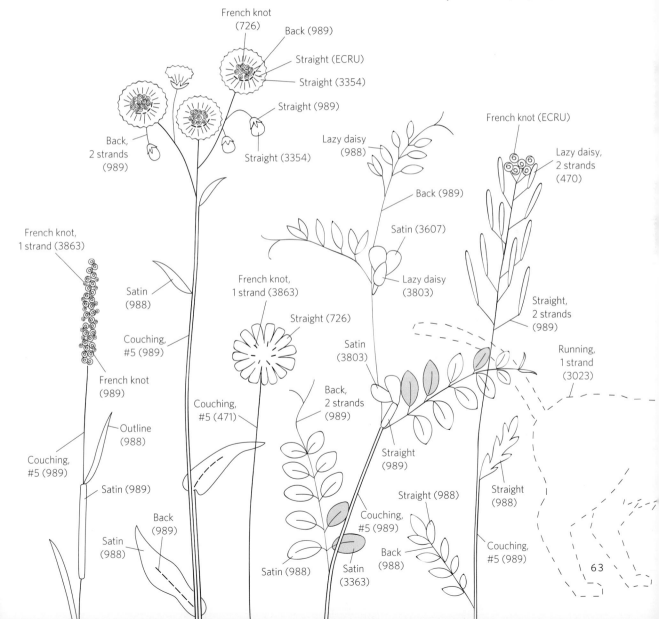

MATERIALS DMC embroidery floss No. 25 (470, 989, 988, 3363, 3354, 3607, 3803, 726, ECRU, 3863, 3023); DMC embroidery floss No. 5 (989, 471)

French knot (726)

Back (989)

Straight (ECRU)

Straight (3354)

Straight (989)

Back, 2 strands (989)

Straight (3354)

Lazy daisy (988)

French knot (ECRU)

Lazy daisy, 2 strands (470)

Back (989)

French knot, 1 strand (3863)

Satin (988)

Satin (3607)

French knot, 1 strand (3863)

Couching, #5 (989)

French knot (989)

Straight (726)

Lazy daisy (3803)

Straight, 2 strands (989)

Running, 1 strand (3023)

Satin (3803)

Outline (988)

Couching, #5 (471)

Back, 2 strands (989)

Couching, #5 (989)

Satin (989)

Straight (989)

Straight (988)

Straight (988)

Back (989)

Straight (988)

Couching, #5 (989)

Satin (988)

Couching, #5 (989)

Satin (988)

Satin (988)

Back (988)

Satin (3363)

63

wild raspberry & mock strawberry page 16

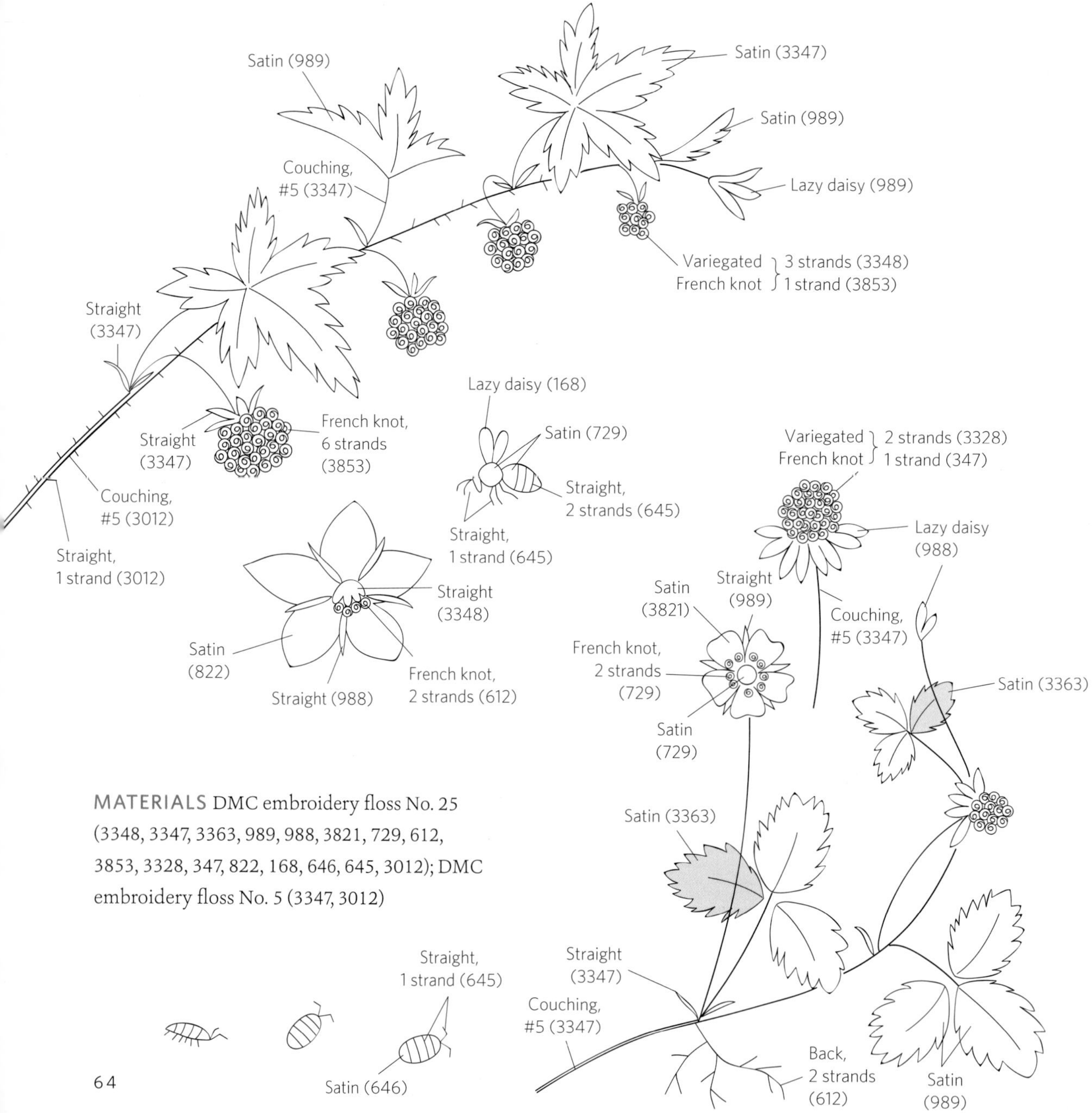
Satin (989)
Satin (3347)
Satin (989)
Lazy daisy (989)
Couching, #5 (3347)
Variegated French knot } 3 strands (3348) 1 strand (3853)
Straight (3347)
Straight (3347)
French knot, 6 strands (3853)
Couching, #5 (3012)
Straight, 1 strand (3012)
Lazy daisy (168)
Satin (729)
Straight, 2 strands (645)
Straight, 1 strand (645)
Variegated French knot } 2 strands (3328) 1 strand (347)
Lazy daisy (988)
Straight (3348)
Satin (822)
Straight (988)
French knot, 2 strands (612)
Satin (3821)
Straight (989)
Couching, #5 (3347)
French knot, 2 strands (729)
Satin (729)
Satin (3363)
Satin (3363)
Straight, 1 strand (645)
Straight (3347)
Couching, #5 (3347)
Satin (646)
Back, 2 strands (612)
Satin (989)

MATERIALS DMC embroidery floss No. 25 (3348, 3347, 3363, 989, 988, 3821, 729, 612, 3853, 3328, 347, 822, 168, 646, 645, 3012); DMC embroidery floss No. 5 (3347, 3012)

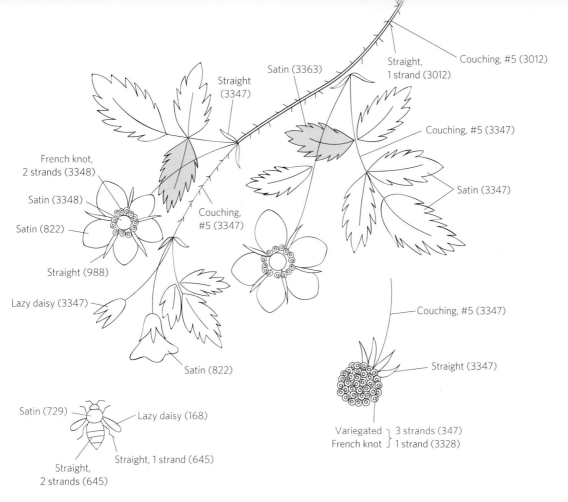

Couching, #5 (3012)

Straight,
1 strand (3012)

Satin (3363)

Straight
(3347)

Couching, #5 (3347)

French knot,
2 strands (3348)

Satin (3348)

Satin (822)

Satin (3347)

Straight (988)

Couching,
#5 (3347)

Lazy daisy (3347)

Couching, #5 (3347)

Straight (3347)

Satin (822)

Satin (729) — Lazy daisy (168)

Straight,
2 strands (645)

Straight, 1 strand (645)

Variegated ⎫ 3 strands (347)
French knot ⎭ 1 strand (3328)

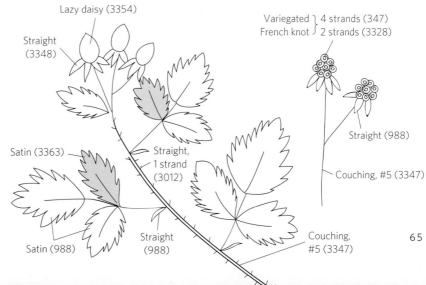

Lazy daisy (3354)

Straight
(3348)

Variegated ⎫ 4 strands (347)
French knot ⎭ 2 strands (3328)

Satin (3363)

Straight,
1 strand
(3012)

Straight (988)

Couching, #5 (3347)

Satin (988)

Straight
(988)

Couching,
#5 (3347)

MATERIALS DMC
embroidery floss No. 25
(3348, 3347, 3363, 988,
729, 3354, 3328, 347,
822, 168, 645, 3012);
DMC embroidery floss
No. 5 (3347, 3012)

rainy days page 18

Satin (794)

Satin (800)

MATERIALS DMC embroidery floss No. 25 (800, 794)

MATERIALS DMC embroidery floss No. 25 (800, 794, 3838, 3807, 155, 210, 3041, 315, 612, 840, 470, 3347); DMC embroidery floss No. 5 (3347)

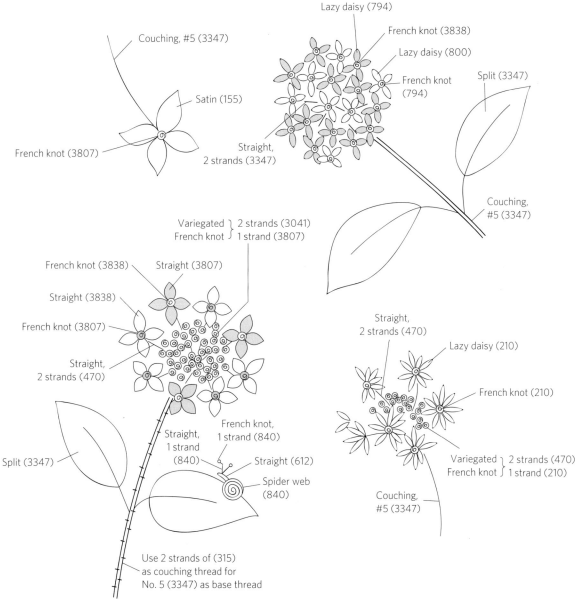

Couching, #5 (3347)

Satin (155)

French knot (3807)

Lazy daisy (794)

French knot (3838)

Lazy daisy (800)

French knot (794)

Split (3347)

Straight, 2 strands (3347)

Couching, #5 (3347)

Variegated French knot } 2 strands (3041) 1 strand (3807)

French knot (3838)   Straight (3807)

Straight (3838)

French knot (3807)

Straight, 2 strands (470)

Split (3347)

Straight, 1 strand (840)

French knot, 1 strand (840)

Straight (612)

Spider web (840)

Use 2 strands of (315) as couching thread for No. 5 (3347) as base thread

Straight, 2 strands (470)

Lazy daisy (210)

French knot (210)

Variegated French knot } 2 strands (470) 1 strand (210)

Couching, #5 (3347)

sunflowers in array page 20

MATERIALS DMC embroidery floss No. 25 (989, 3347, 3363, 3819, 17, 3821, 612, 3045, 3862, 839, 844, 3023); DMC embroidery floss No. 5 (989)

NOTES All the leaves are worked in satin stitch. All the flower petals are worked in lazy daisy stitch. Use the same thread color for all the flower centers and all the stems.

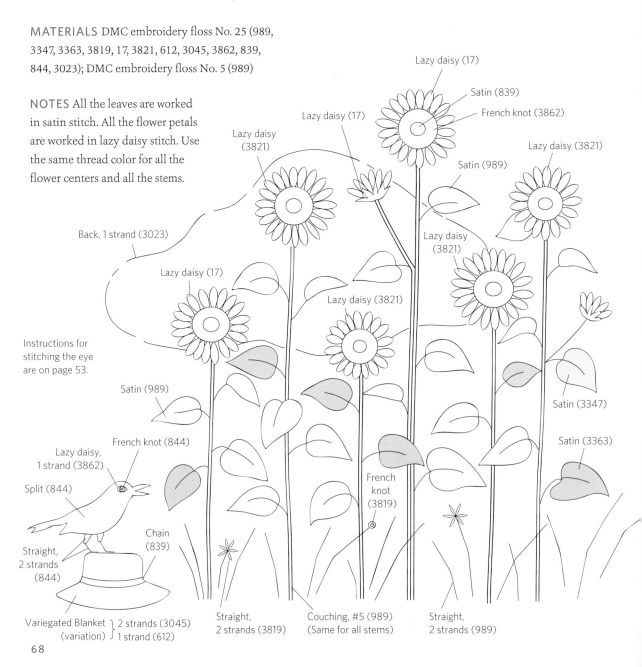

Lazy daisy (17)

Satin (839)

French knot (3862)

Lazy daisy (17)

Lazy daisy (3821)

Lazy daisy (3821)

Satin (989)

Back, 1 strand (3023)

Lazy daisy (3821)

Lazy daisy (17)

Lazy daisy (3821)

Instructions for stitching the eye are on page 53.

Satin (3347)

Satin (989)

Satin (3363)

French knot (844)

Lazy daisy, 1 strand (3862)

Split (844)

French knot (3819)

Straight, 2 strands (844)

Chain (839)

Variegated Blanket (variation) } 2 strands (3045) 1 strand (612)

Straight, 2 strands (3819)

Couching, #5 (989) (Same for all stems)

Straight, 2 strands (989)

MATERIALS DMC embroidery floss No. 25
(989, 3347, 3363, 3819, 17, 3821, 3862, 839,
3023); DMC embroidery floss No. 5 (989)

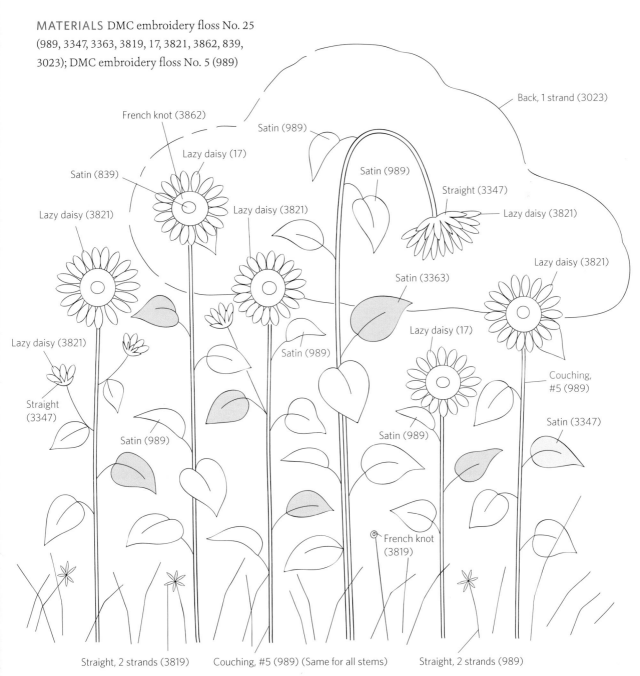

Back, 1 strand (3023)

French knot (3862)

Satin (989)

Lazy daisy (17)

Satin (989)

Satin (839)

Straight (3347)

Lazy daisy (3821)

Lazy daisy (3821)

Lazy daisy (3821)

Lazy daisy (3821)

Satin (3363)

Lazy daisy (17)

Satin (989)

Lazy daisy (3821)

Straight (3347)

Couching, #5 (989)

Satin (989)

Satin (989)

Satin (3347)

Satin (989)

French knot (3819)

Straight, 2 strands (3819)   Couching, #5 (989) (Same for all stems)   Straight, 2 strands (989)

flowering grasses page 22

MATERIALS DMC embroidery floss
No. 25 (989, 3347, 3346, 471, 470, 729,
436, 612, 3023, 645); DMC embroidery
floss No. 5 (989, 3347, 3346)

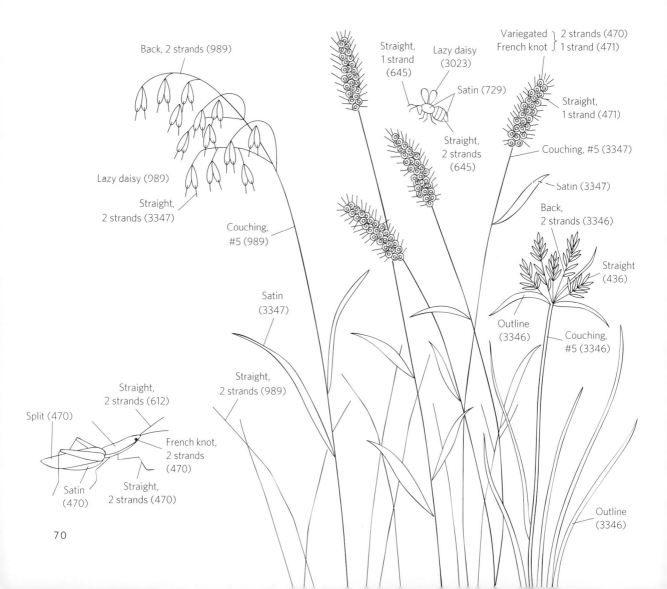

Back, 2 strands (989)

Straight,
1 strand
(645)

Lazy daisy
(3023)

Satin (729)

Variegated ⎱ 2 strands (470)
French knot ⎰ 1 strand (471)

Straight,
1 strand (471)

Couching, #5 (3347)

Straight,
2 strands
(645)

Satin (3347)

Back,
2 strands (3346)

Lazy daisy (989)

Straight,
2 strands (3347)

Straight
(436)

Couching,
#5 (989)

Outline
(3346)

Couching,
#5 (3346)

Satin
(3347)

Straight,
2 strands (989)

Split (470)

Straight,
2 strands (612)

French knot,
2 strands
(470)

Satin
(470)

Straight,
2 strands (470)

Outline
(3346)

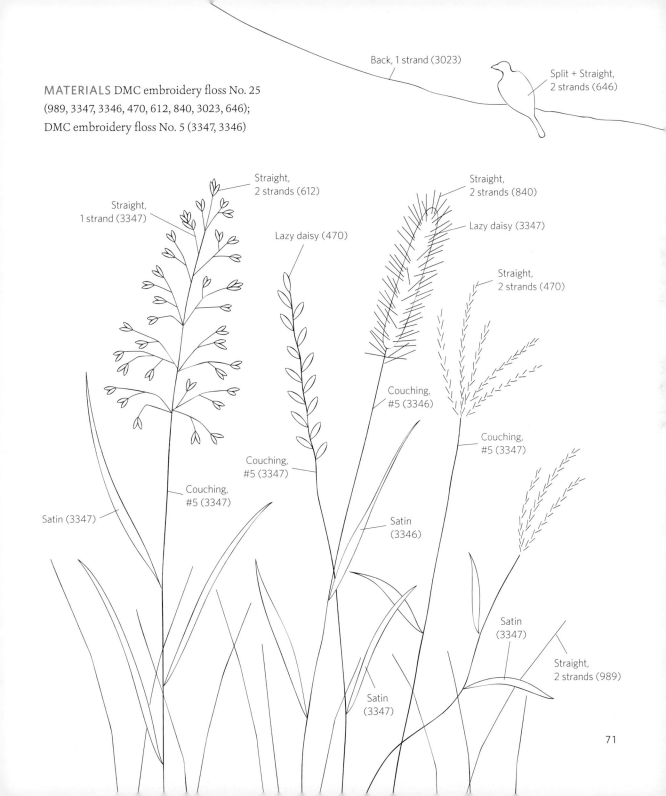

MATERIALS DMC embroidery floss No. 25
(989, 3347, 3346, 470, 612, 840, 3023, 646);
DMC embroidery floss No. 5 (3347, 3346)

Back, 1 strand (3023)

Split + Straight,
2 strands (646)

Straight,
2 strands (612)

Straight,
1 strand (3347)

Lazy daisy (470)

Straight,
2 strands (840)

Lazy daisy (3347)

Straight,
2 strands (470)

Couching,
#5 (3346)

Couching,
#5 (3347)

Couching,
#5 (3347)

Couching,
#5 (3347)

Satin (3347)

Satin
(3346)

Satin
(3347)

Satin
(3347)

Straight,
2 strands (989)

Satin
(3347)

in the corners of the garden page 24

MATERIALS DMC embroidery
floss No. 25 (369, 471, 988, 320,
3346, 3822, 3820, 844, 3860); DMC
embroidery floss No. 5 (471, 841)

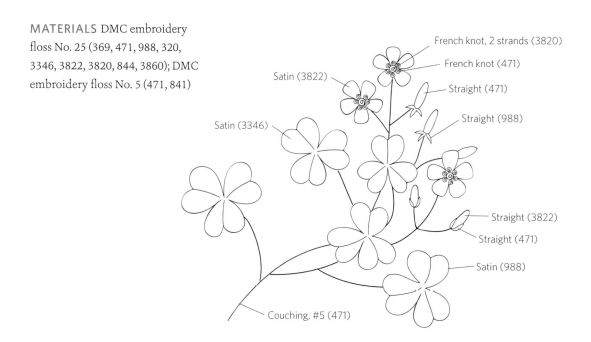

French knot, 2 strands (3820)
French knot (471)
Satin (3822)
Straight (471)
Straight (988)
Satin (3346)
Straight (3822)
Straight (471)
Satin (988)
Couching, #5 (471)

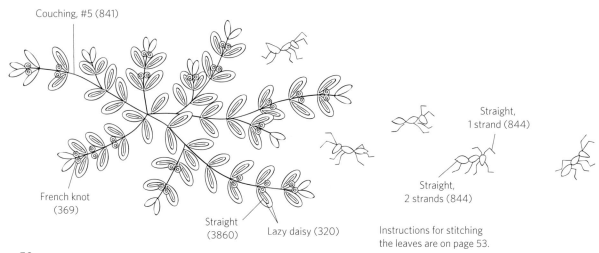

Couching, #5 (841)
Straight,
1 strand (844)
Straight,
2 strands (844)
French knot
(369)
Straight
(3860)
Lazy daisy (320)

Instructions for stitching
the leaves are on page 53.

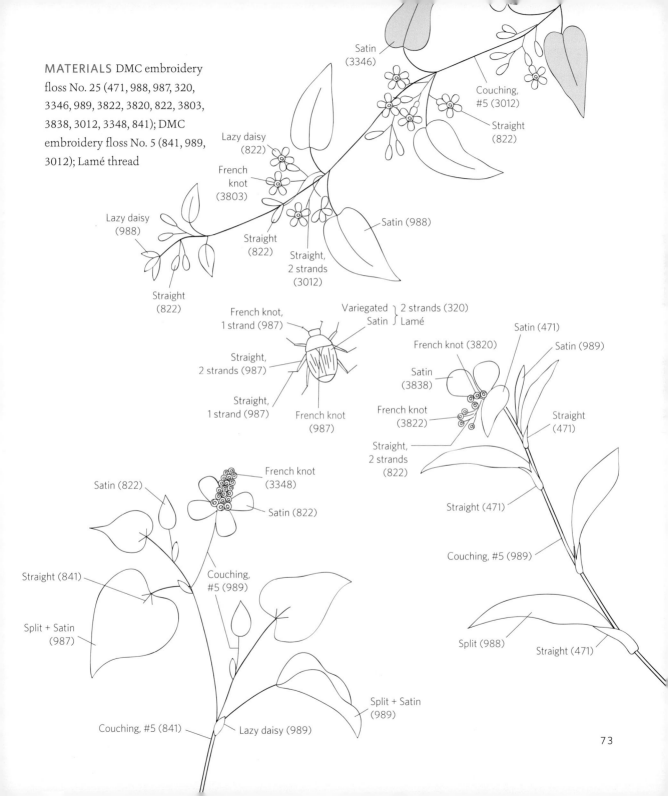

MATERIALS DMC embroidery floss No. 25 (471, 988, 987, 320, 3346, 989, 3822, 3820, 822, 3803, 3838, 3012, 3348, 841); DMC embroidery floss No. 5 (841, 989, 3012); Lamé thread

Satin (3346)

Couching, #5 (3012)

Straight (822)

Lazy daisy (822)

French knot (3803)

Lazy daisy (988)

Straight (822)

Straight (822)

Straight, 2 strands (3012)

Satin (988)

French knot, 1 strand (987)

Variegated Satin } 2 strands (320) } Lamé

Satin (471)

Satin (989)

French knot (3820)

Satin (3838)

Straight, 2 strands (987)

French knot (3822)

Straight (471)

Straight, 1 strand (987)

French knot (987)

Straight, 2 strands (822)

Straight (471)

French knot (3348)

Satin (822)

Satin (822)

Couching, #5 (989)

Straight (841)

Split + Satin (987)

Couching, #5 (989)

Couching, #5 (841)

Lazy daisy (989)

Split + Satin (989)

Split (988)

Straight (471)

73

summer's butterflies page 26

MATERIALS DMC embroidery floss
No. 25 (3078, 976, 3023, 646, 844,
156); Wire (Bare floral wire, 30 gauge)

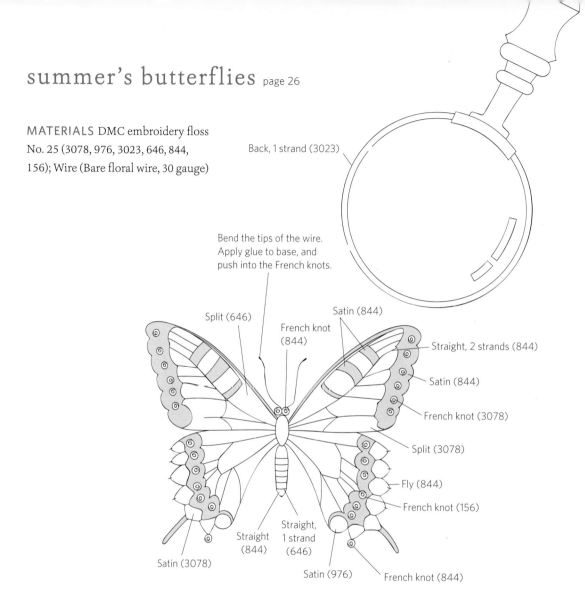

Back, 1 strand (3023)

Bend the tips of the wire.
Apply glue to base, and
push into the French knots.

Split (646)

French knot
(844)

Satin (844)

Straight, 2 strands (844)

Satin (844)

French knot (3078)

Split (3078)

Fly (844)

French knot (156)

Satin (3078)

Straight
(844)

Straight,
1 strand
(646)

Satin (976)

French knot (844)

MATERIALS DMC embroidery floss No.
25 (822, 3078, 976, 420, 434, 646, 844, 350,
156, 839); Wire (Bare floral wire, 30 gauge)

Split (156)

Straight (420)

French knot
(844)

Straight
(156)

Straight (844)

French knot (844)

Satin (434)

Satin (350)

Straight (844)

Straight
(844)

Straight,
1 strand (646)

Satin (844)

French knot,
2 strands (3078)

French knot (976)

Straight (844)

Split
(3078)

Straight (646)

Straight (844)

Straight,
1 strand (646)

Bend the tips of the wire.
Apply glue to base, and
push into the French knots.

For all eyes,
French knot
(844)

Straight
(844)

Satin + Split (434)

Straight, 1 strand (839)

French knot (844)

Split (976)

Split (434)

Straight (434)

Straight
(844)

Straight, 1 strand (434)

Straight,
2 strands (3078)

Satin (844)

French knot (844)

Straight (844)

Straight,
1 strand (646)

Split (822)

Straight
(844)

Straight, 1 strand (646)

autumn paths page 30

MATERIALS DMC embroidery floss
No. 25 (989, 988, 3363, 320, 3772, 554,
3688, 3803, 155, 168, 844, 729); DMC
embroidery floss No. 5 (368, 989, 3012)

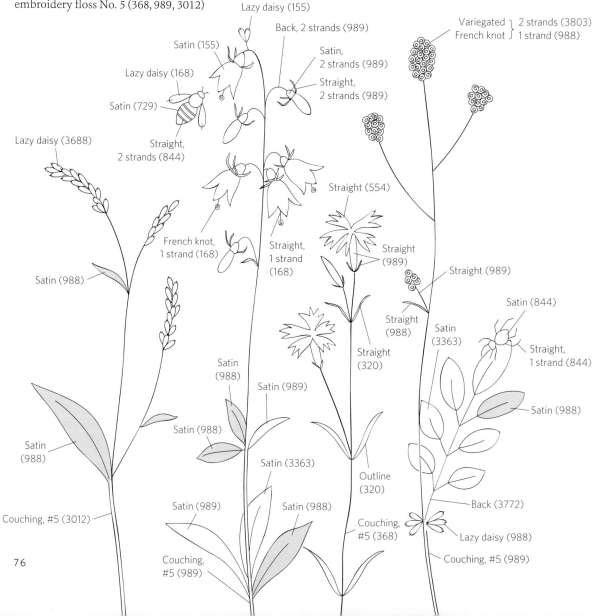

Lazy daisy (155)

Back, 2 strands (989)

Satin (155)

Satin,
2 strands (989)

Lazy daisy (168)

Straight,
2 strands (989)

Satin (729)

Variegated ⎫ 2 strands (3803)
French knot ⎰ 1 strand (988)

Straight,
2 strands (844)

Lazy daisy (3688)

Straight (554)

Satin (988)

French knot,
1 strand (168)

Straight,
1 strand
(168)

Straight
(989)

Straight (989)

Satin (844)

Straight (988)

Satin
(3363)

Straight,
1 strand (844)

Satin
(988)

Satin (989)

Satin (988)

Satin (988)

Straight
(320)

Satin
(988)

Satin (3363)

Satin (989)

Satin (988)

Outline
(320)

Back (3772)

Couching, #5 (3012)

Couching,
#5 (368)

Lazy daisy (988)

Couching, #5 (989)

Satin
(988)

Couching,
#5 (989)

Couching,
#5 (989)

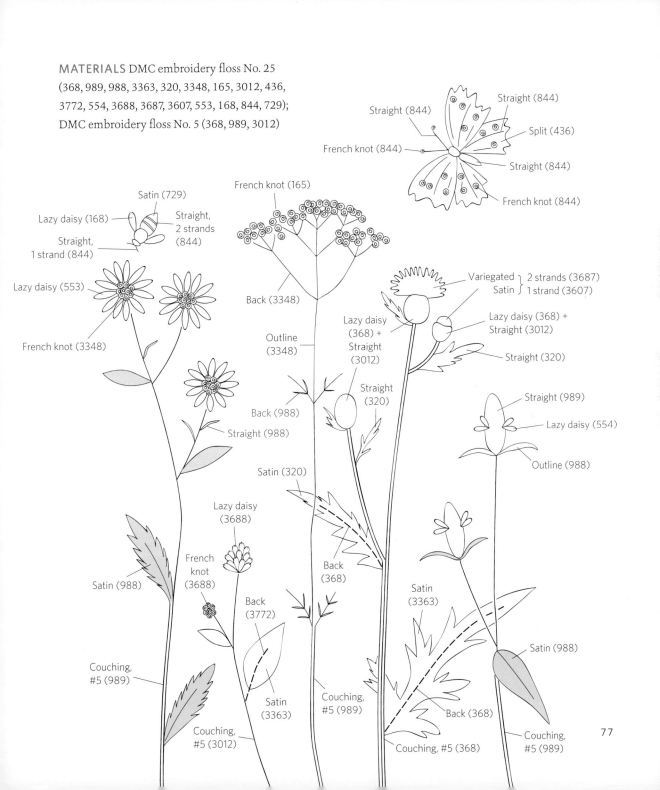

MATERIALS DMC embroidery floss No. 25
(368, 989, 988, 3363, 320, 3348, 165, 3012, 436,
3772, 554, 3688, 3687, 3607, 553, 168, 844, 729);
DMC embroidery floss No. 5 (368, 989, 3012)

Straight (844)

Straight (844)

Split (436)

French knot (844)

Straight (844)

French knot (844)

Satin (729)

Lazy daisy (168)

Straight,
2 strands
(844)

Straight,
1 strand (844)

French knot (165)

Lazy daisy (553)

Back (3348)

Variegated ⎱ 2 strands (3687)
Satin ⎰ 1 strand (3607)

Lazy daisy
(368) +
Straight
(3012)

Lazy daisy (368) +
Straight (3012)

Straight (320)

French knot (3348)

Outline
(3348)

Straight
(320)

Straight (989)

Lazy daisy (554)

Back (988)

Outline (988)

Straight (988)

Satin (320)

Lazy daisy
(3688)

Back
(368)

Satin (988)

French
knot
(3688)

Back
(3772)

Satin
(3363)

Satin (988)

Couching,
#5 (989)

Back (368)

Couching,
#5 (3012)

Satin
(3363)

Couching,
#5 (989)

Couching, #5 (368)

Couching,
#5 (989)

77

colorful changing leaves page 32

MATERIALS DMC embroidery floss No.
25 (165, 833, 729, 420, 350, 921, 822, 471)

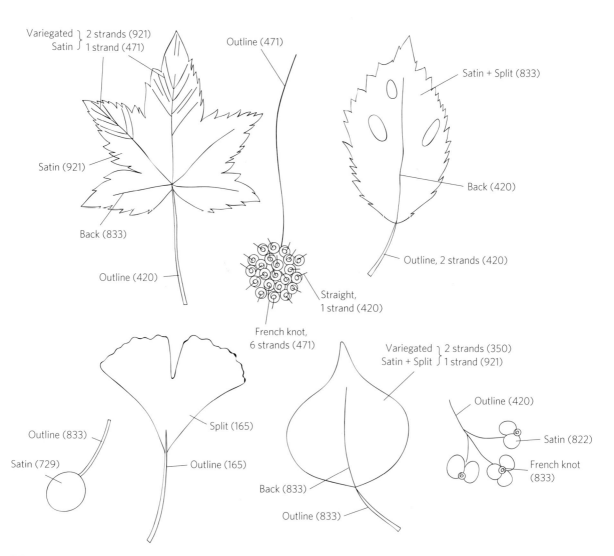

Variegated } 2 strands (921)
Satin } 1 strand (471)

Outline (471)

Satin + Split (833)

Satin (921)

Back (833)

Back (420)

Outline (420)

Outline, 2 strands (420)

Straight,
1 strand (420)

French knot,
6 strands (471)

Outline (833)

Satin (729)

Split (165)

Outline (165)

Variegated } 2 strands (350)
Satin + Split } 1 strand (921)

Outline (420)

Satin (822)

French knot
(833)

Back (833)

Outline (833)

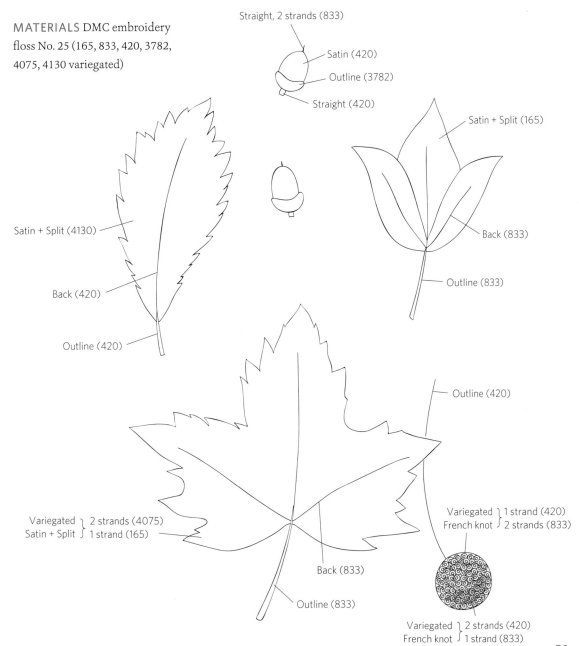

MATERIALS DMC embroidery
floss No. 25 (165, 833, 420, 3782,
4075, 4130 variegated)

Straight, 2 strands (833)

Satin (420)

Outline (3782)

Straight (420)

Satin + Split (165)

Back (833)

Outline (833)

Satin + Split (4130)

Back (420)

Outline (420)

Outline (420)

Variegated } 1 strand (420)
French knot } 2 strands (833)

Variegated } 2 strands (4075)
Satin + Split } 1 strand (165)

Back (833)

Outline (833)

Variegated } 2 strands (420)
French knot } 1 strand (833)

forest combing page 34

MATERIALS DMC embroidery
floss No. 25 (3866, 738, 437, 436,
435, 420, 840, 612, 677, 3822,
921, 350, 647, 645, 844); DMC
embroidery floss No. 5 (3046)

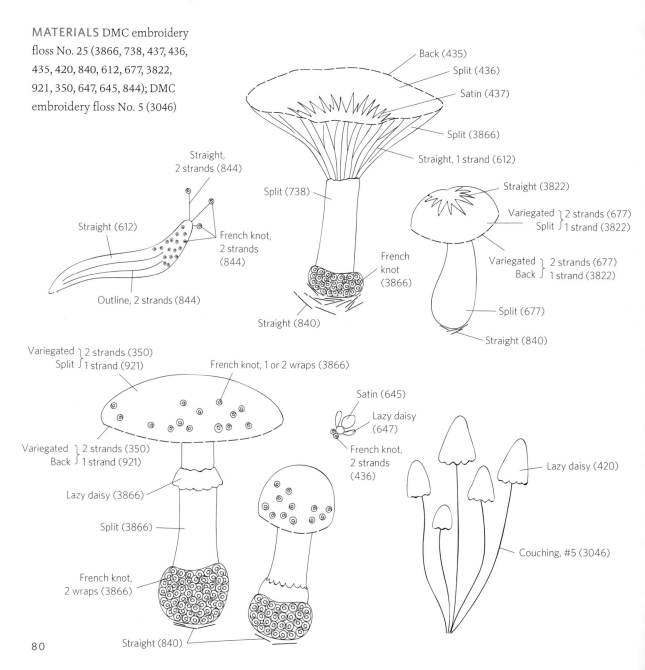

Back (435)

Split (436)

Satin (437)

Split (3866)

Straight, 1 strand (612)

Split (738)

French
knot
(3866)

Straight (840)

Straight,
2 strands (844)

Straight (612)

French knot,
2 strands
(844)

Outline, 2 strands (844)

Straight (3822)

Variegated } 2 strands (677)
Split } 1 strand (3822)

Variegated } 2 strands (677)
Back } 1 strand (3822)

Split (677)

Straight (840)

Variegated } 2 strands (350)
Split } 1 strand (921)

French knot, 1 or 2 wraps (3866)

Satin (645)

Lazy daisy
(647)

French knot,
2 strands
(436)

Lazy daisy (420)

Variegated } 2 strands (350)
Back } 1 strand (921)

Lazy daisy (3866)

Split (3866)

French knot,
2 wraps (3866)

Couching, #5 (3046)

Straight (840)

MATERIALS DMC embroidery floss No. 25 (3866, 738, 436, 420, 840, 3743, 209, 340, 647, 3778); DMC embroidery floss No. 5 (3046)

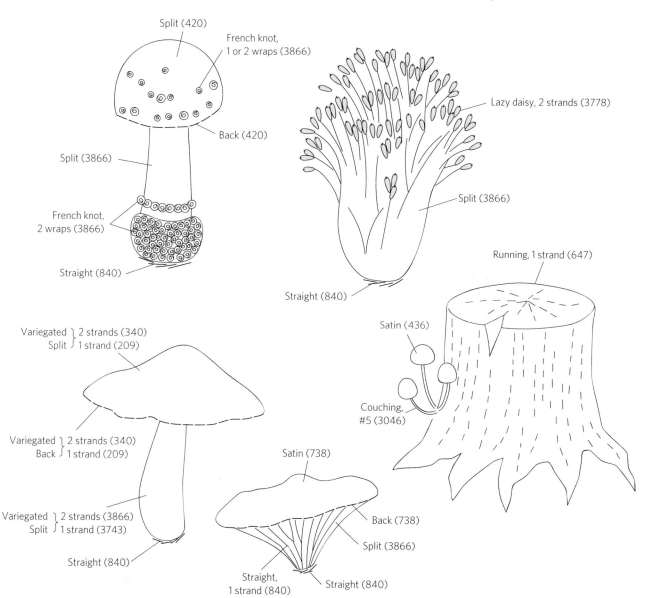

Split (420)

French knot,
1 or 2 wraps (3866)

Back (420)

Split (3866)

French knot,
2 wraps (3866)

Straight (840)

Lazy daisy, 2 strands (3778)

Split (3866)

Straight (840)

Running, 1 strand (647)

Satin (436)

Couching,
#5 (3046)

Variegated } 2 strands (340)
Split } 1 strand (209)

Variegated } 2 strands (340)
Back } 1 strand (209)

Variegated } 2 strands (3866)
Split } 1 strand (3743)

Straight (840)

Satin (738)

Back (738)

Split (3866)

Straight,
1 strand (840)

Straight (840)

the opposite bank of the canal page 36

Back, 2 strands (640)

MATERIALS DMC embroidery floss No. 25 (833, 301, 3023, 640, 645, ECRU); Art Fiber Endo linen embroidery thread (L903, L910); Art Fiber Endo tulle scraps (green), as needed

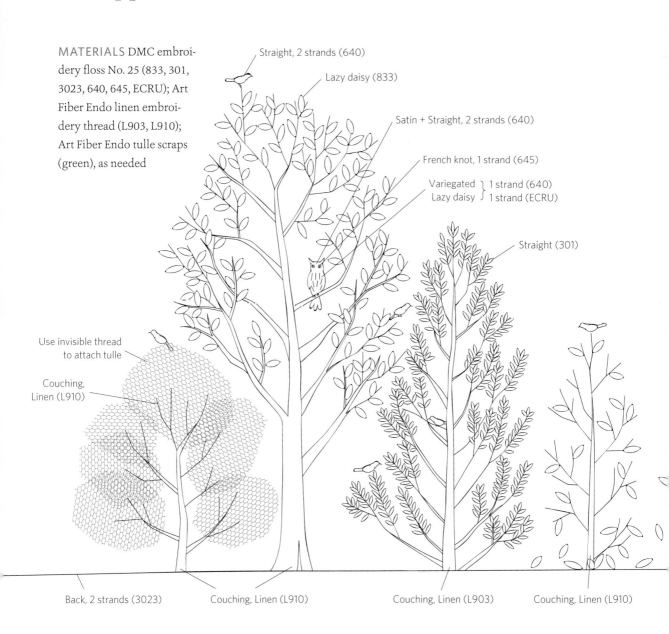

Straight, 2 strands (640)

Lazy daisy (833)

Satin + Straight, 2 strands (640)

French knot, 1 strand (645)

Variegated } 1 strand (640)
Lazy daisy } 1 strand (ECRU)

Straight (301)

Use invisible thread to attach tulle

Couching, Linen (L910)

Back, 2 strands (3023)

Couching, Linen (L910)

Couching, Linen (L903)

Couching, Linen (L910)

MATERIALS DMC embroidery floss No. 25 (833,
782, 301, 932, 3023, 640, 645, ECRU); Art Fiber
Endo linen embroidery thread (L903, L910); Art
Fiber Endo tulle scraps (green), as needed.

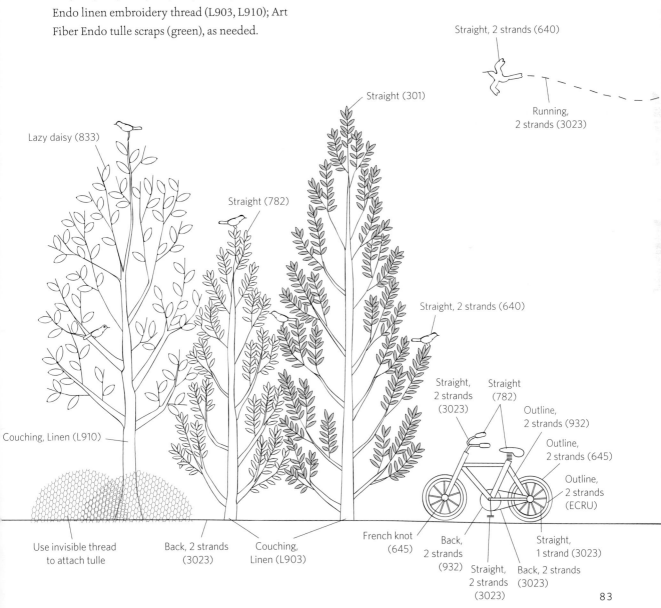

Straight, 2 strands (640)

Running,
2 strands (3023)

Straight (301)

Lazy daisy (833)

Straight (782)

Straight, 2 strands (640)

Straight,
2 strands
(3023)

Straight
(782)

Outline,
2 strands (932)

Outline,
2 strands (645)

Outline,
2 strands
(ECRU)

Couching, Linen (L910)

Use invisible thread
to attach tulle

Back, 2 strands
(3023)

Couching,
Linen (L903)

French knot
(645)

Back,
2 strands
(932)

Straight,
2 strands
(3023)

Back, 2 strands
(3023)

Straight,
1 strand (3023)

83

bird watching page 38

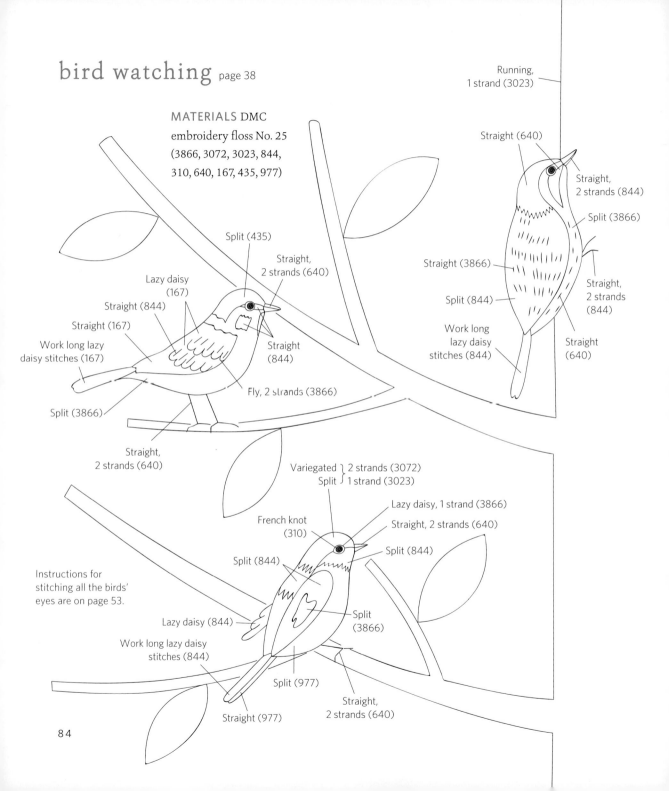

MATERIALS DMC
embroidery floss No. 25
(3866, 3072, 3023, 844,
310, 640, 167, 435, 977)

Running,
1 strand (3023)

Straight (640)

Straight,
2 strands (844)

Split (3866)

Straight (3866)

Split (844)

Straight,
2 strands
(844)

Work long
lazy daisy
stitches (844)

Straight
(640)

Split (435)

Straight,
2 strands (640)

Lazy daisy
(167)

Straight (844)

Straight (167)

Work long lazy
daisy stitches (167)

Straight
(844)

Split (3866)

Fly, 2 strands (3866)

Straight,
2 strands (640)

Variegated } 2 strands (3072)
Split } 1 strand (3023)

Lazy daisy, 1 strand (3866)

Straight, 2 strands (640)

French knot
(310)

Split (844)

Split (844)

Split
(3866)

Lazy daisy (844)

Instructions for
stitching all the birds'
eyes are on page 53.

Work long lazy daisy
stitches (844)

Split (977)

Straight (977)

Straight,
2 strands (640)

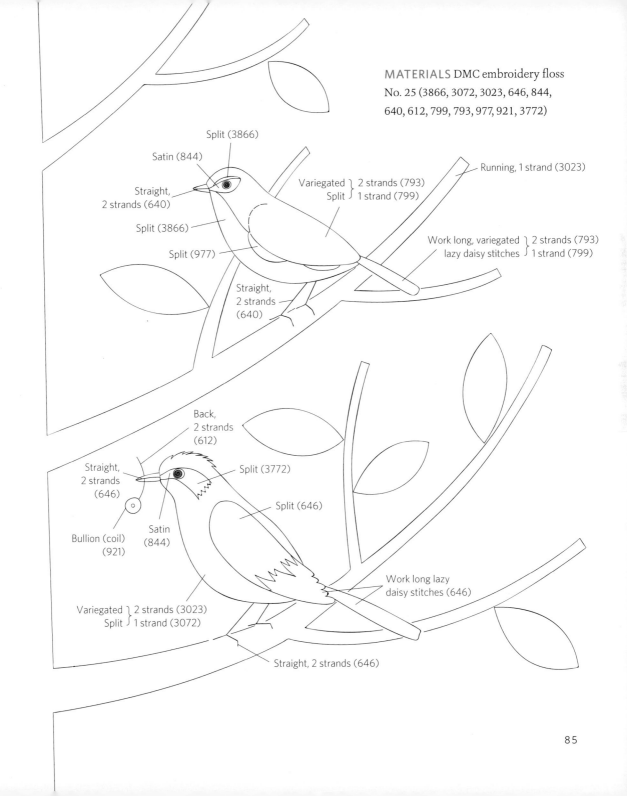

MATERIALS DMC embroidery floss
No. 25 (3866, 3072, 3023, 646, 844, 640, 612, 799, 793, 977, 921, 3772)

Split (3866)

Satin (844)

Straight, 2 strands (640)

Split (3866)

Split (977)

Variegated { 2 strands (793)
Split { 1 strand (799)

Running, 1 strand (3023)

Work long, variegated { 2 strands (793)
lazy daisy stitches { 1 strand (799)

Straight, 2 strands (640)

Back, 2 strands (612)

Straight, 2 strands (646)

Split (3772)

Split (646)

Bullion (coil) (921)

Satin (844)

Variegated { 2 strands (3023)
Split { 1 strand (3072)

Work long lazy daisy stitches (646)

Straight, 2 strands (646)

85

mistletoe page 40

MATERIALS DMC embroidery floss No. 25 (3012,
368, 3347, 11, 921); DMC embroidery floss No. 5
(612); Art Fiber Endo linen embroidery thread (L204)

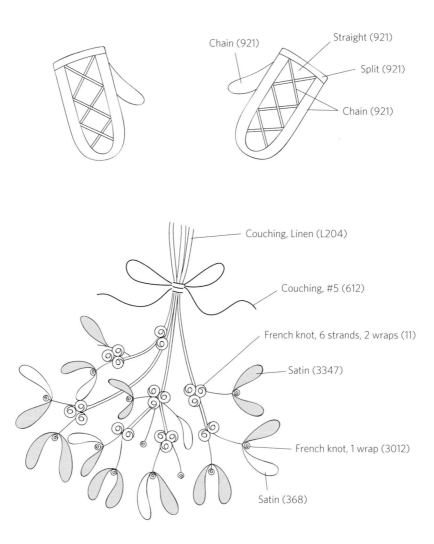

Chain (921)

Straight (921)

Split (921)

Chain (921)

Couching, Linen (L204)

Couching, #5 (612)

French knot, 6 strands, 2 wraps (11)

Satin (3347)

French knot, 1 wrap (3012)

Satin (368)

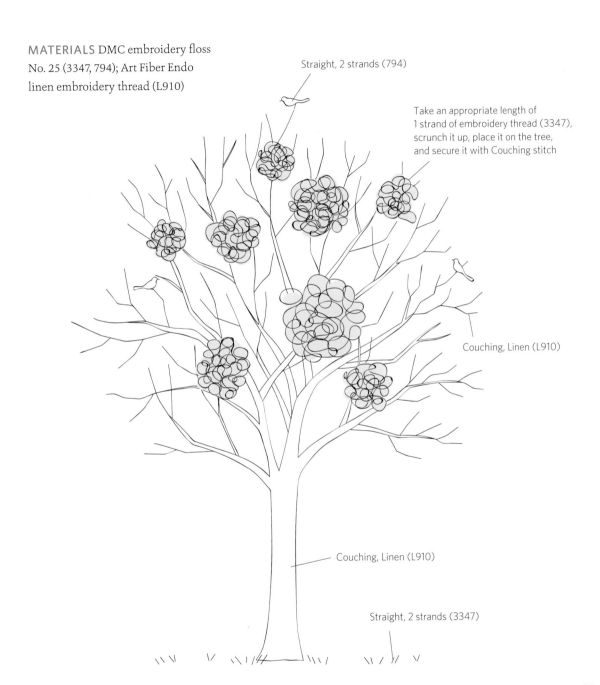

MATERIALS DMC embroidery floss
No. 25 (3347, 794); Art Fiber Endo
linen embroidery thread (L910)

Straight, 2 strands (794)

Take an appropriate length of
1 strand of embroidery thread (3347),
scrunch it up, place it on the tree,
and secure it with Couching stitch

Couching, Linen (L910)

Couching, Linen (L910)

Straight, 2 strands (3347)

collecting materials page 42

DMC embroidery floss No. 25 (612, 841,
3772, 320, 987, 3363, 3768, 3023); DMC
embroidery floss No. 5 (612); Art Fiber
Endo linen embroidery thread (L403)

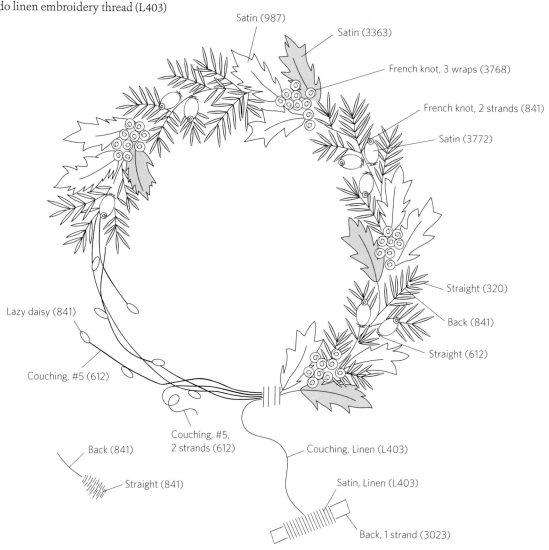

Satin (987)

Satin (3363)

French knot, 3 wraps (3768)

French knot, 2 strands (841)

Satin (3772)

Straight (320)

Back (841)

Straight (612)

Lazy daisy (841)

Couching, #5 (612)

Couching, #5,
2 strands (612)

Couching, Linen (L403)

Back (841)

Straight (841)

Satin, Linen (L403)

Back, 1 strand (3023)

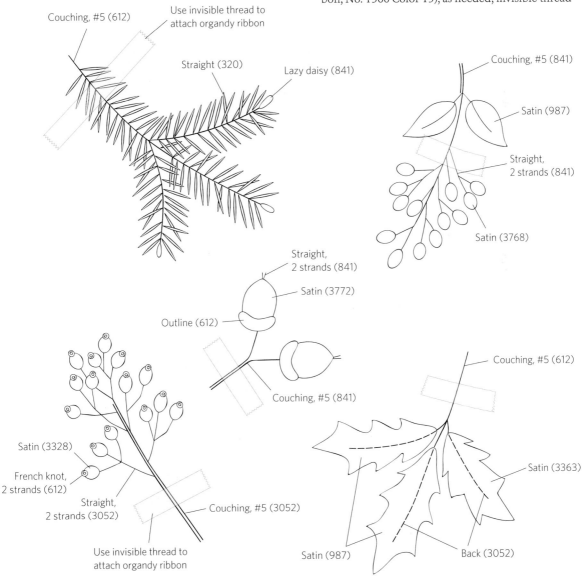

MATERIALS DMC embroidery floss No. 25 (612, 841, 3772, 320, 987, 3052, 3363, 3328, 3768); DMC embroidery floss No. 5 (612, 841, 3052); 5-mm-wide organdy ribbon scraps (MOKUBA embroidery ribbon, No. 1500 Color 15), as needed; invisible thread

Couching, #5 (612)

Use invisible thread to attach organdy ribbon

Straight (320)

Lazy daisy (841)

Couching, #5 (841)

Satin (987)

Straight, 2 strands (841)

Satin (3768)

Straight, 2 strands (841)

Satin (3772)

Outline (612)

Couching, #5 (841)

Satin (3328)

French knot, 2 strands (612)

Straight, 2 strands (3052)

Couching, #5 (3052)

Use invisible thread to attach organdy ribbon

Couching, #5 (612)

Satin (3363)

Satin (987)

Back (3052)

the world of mosses page 44

MATERIALS DMC embroidery floss No. 25
(470, 368, 320, 988, 3347, 3046, 3772, 3023); Art
Fiber Endo linen embroidery thread (L904);
polyester organdy scraps (green), double-sided
fusible interfacing scraps, as needed

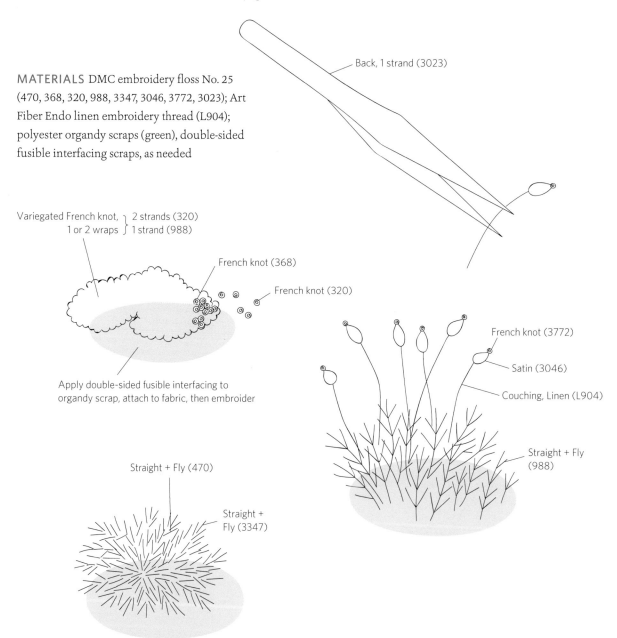

Back, 1 strand (3023)

Variegated French knot,　⎱ 2 strands (320)
1 or 2 wraps　⎰ 1 strand (988)

French knot (368)

French knot (320)

Apply double-sided fusible interfacing to
organdy scrap, attach to fabric, then embroider

French knot (3772)

Satin (3046)

Couching, Linen (L904)

Straight + Fly
(988)

Straight + Fly (470)

Straight +
Fly (3347)

MATERIALS DMC embroidery floss No. 25 (471, 368, 320, 3347, 3772, 3023); Art Fiber Endo linen embroidery thread (L908); polyester organdy scraps (green), double-sided fusible interfacing scraps, as needed

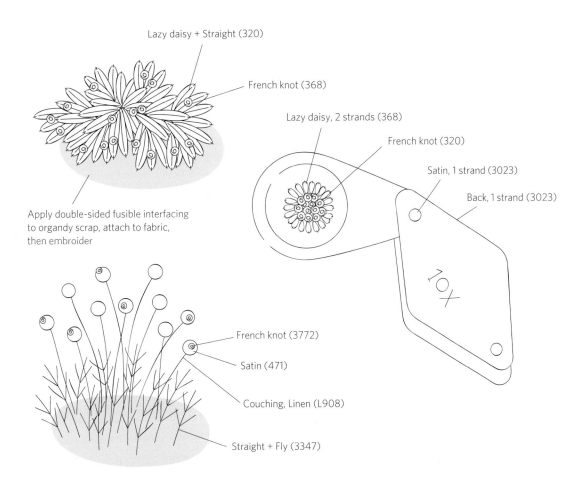

Lazy daisy + Straight (320)

French knot (368)

Apply double-sided fusible interfacing to organdy scrap, attach to fabric, then embroider

Lazy daisy, 2 strands (368)

French knot (320)

Satin, 1 strand (3023)

Back, 1 strand (3023)

10X

French knot (3772)

Satin (471)

Couching, Linen (L908)

Straight + Fly (3347)

objects that are rather ordinary but still special page 46

MATERIALS DMC embroidery floss No. 25 (01, 648, 646, 535, 844, 422, 407, 07, 08, 3346); DMC embroidery floss No. 5 (646, 989); 5-mm-wide organdy ribbon scrap (MOKUBA embroidery ribbon, No. 1500 Color 15); invisible thread

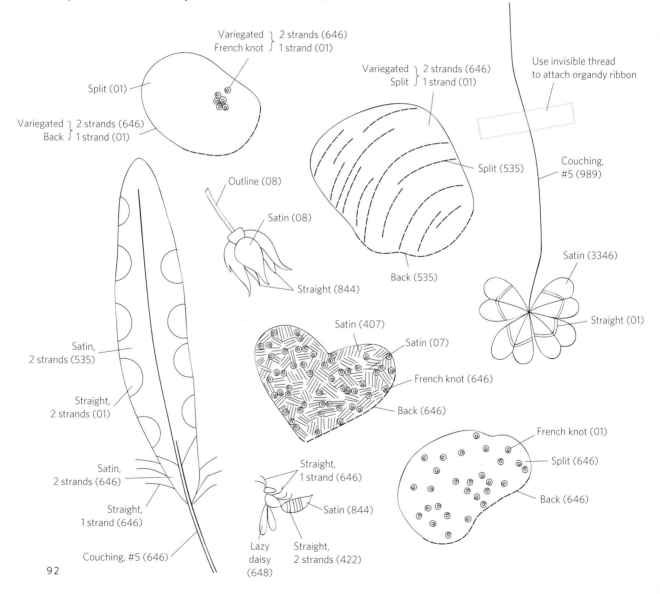

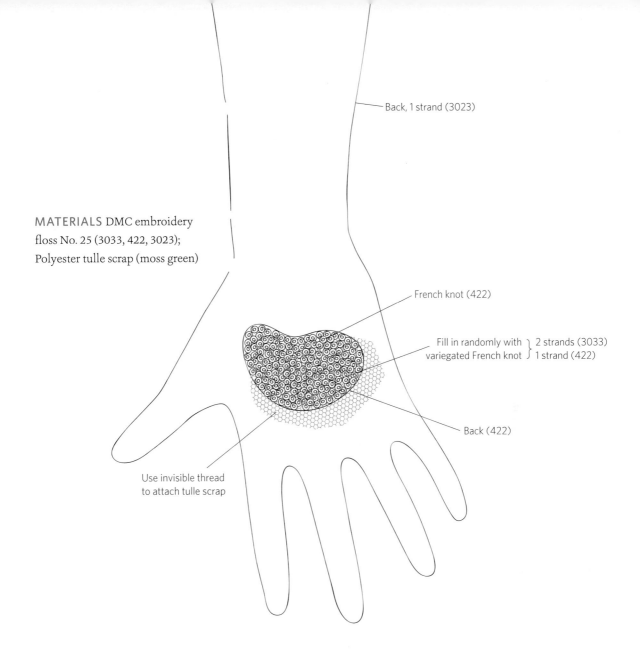

Back, 1 strand (3023)

MATERIALS DMC embroidery
floss No. 25 (3033, 422, 3023);
Polyester tulle scrap (moss green)

French knot (422)

Fill in randomly with } 2 strands (3033)
variegated French knot } 1 strand (422)

Back (422)

Use invisible thread
to attach tulle scrap

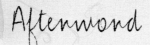

Afterword

When I was a child and would walk around the neighborhood where I lived, I'd find shards of pottery. I'd marvel at the discovery of white shells in the garden soil.

Now it's a leafy and green residential area, but a very long time ago, it was the seashore where the Jomon people lived.

The stones and pebbles that I picked up along my walks were probably there under the feet of those ancient people, all those years ago.

When I imagine them, in this same place, looking up at the same sky, it feels as though I might be swallowed up by the great beyond.

Here is a favorite quote of mine:

> Don't hurry, don't worry
>
> We are only here for a short visit
>
> So be sure to stop and smell the flowers.
>
> —Walter Hagen

As we walk along on our way, let's enjoy the flowers in bloom.

KAZUKO AOKI designs embroidery patterns based on her sketches of garden and field flowers that she has encountered in her travels as well as those she finds in her own garden. The endearing natural beauty and delight of her numerous charming projects resonate deeply with many people. More than just a craftsperson, she considers herself a horticulturalist, passionately engaged in her studies. Aoki's books include *The Embroidered Garden* and *Embroidered Garden Flowers*.

Roost Books
An imprint of Shambhala Publications, Inc.
2129 13th Street
Boulder, Colorado 80302
www.shambhala.com

© 2018 by Kazuko Aoki/Bunka Publishing Bureau
Originally published as *Aoki Kazuko no shishu Sanpo no techo* by Kazuko Aoki in Japan in 2018 by Bunka Publishing Bureau (Bunka Shuppan Kyoku), Tokyo.

Translation © 2020 by Shambhala Publications, Inc.
Translation by Allison Markin Powell

Bunka Publishing Bureau (Bunka Shuppan Kyoku) Staff Credits
Publisher: Sunao Onuma
Book Design: Mihoko Amano
Photography: Josui Yasuda (for Bunka Shuppan Kyoku)
Tracing: (day studio) Satomi Dairaku
DTP: Bunka Fototype
Proofreader: Emiko Horiguchi
Editor: Yoko Osawa
Special thanks to Harumi Koda

9 8 7 6 5

Printed in China

Shambhala Publications makes every effort to print on acid-free, recycled paper.

Roost Books is distributed worldwide by Penguin Random House, Inc., and its subsidiaries.

LIBRARY OF CONGRESS CATALOGING-IN-PUBLICATION DATA

NAMES: Aoki, Kazuko, 1953– author.
Title: Embroidered wild flowers: patterns inspired by field and forest / [Kazuko Aoki].
OTHER TITLES: Aoki Kazuko no shishū sanpo no techō. English
DESCRIPTION: First English edition. | Boulder: Roost Books, 2020.
IDENTIFIERS: LCCN 2019025775 | ISBN 9781611808018 (trade paperback)
SUBJECTS: LCSH: Embroidery—Patterns. | Decoration and ornament—Plant forms.
CLASSIFICATION: LCC TT773 .A6613 2020 | DDC 746.44/041–dc23
LC record available at https://lccn.loc.gov/2019025775